NO CAUSE OF OFFENCE

A VIRGINIA FAMILY OF UNION LOYALISTS CONFRONTS THE CIVIL WAR

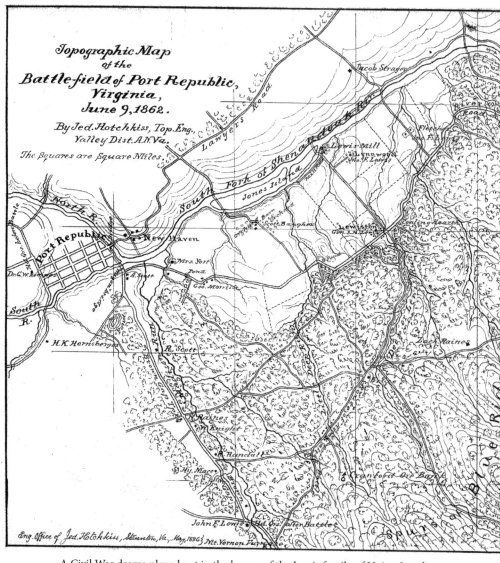

A Civil War drama played out in the homes of the Lewis family of Union Loyalists beside the banks of Virginia's Shenandoah River. Confederate Gen. Stonewall Jackson was hosted at Lewiston, above right of center, eight days before the Battle of Port Republic sent the family fleeing across the river to the home of Jacob Strayer. John F. Lewis kept dozens of Union Loyalists out of the Confederate Army by employing them at his iron operation, Mount Vernon Furnace, bottom center.

No Cause of Offence

A Virginia Family of Union Loyalists Confronts the Civil War

LEWIS F. FISHER

Maverick Publishing Company

MAVERICK PUBLISHING COMPANY
P.O. Box 6355, San Antonio, Texas 78209

Library of Congress Cataloging-in-Publication Data

Fisher, Lewis F.
  No cause of offence : a Virginia family of Union loyalists confronts the Civil War/Lewis F. Fisher.
    p. cm.
Includes bibliographical references and index.
  ISBN 978-1-893271-61-6
  1. Lewis, Samuel Hance, 1794–1869. 2. Lewis, Samuel Hance, 1794–1869–Family. 3. Unionists
(United States Civil War)–Virginia–Rockingham County–Biography. 4. Politicians–Virginia–
Rockingham County–Biography. 5. Republican Party (U.S. : 1854–)–Biography. 6. Rockingham
County (Va.)–Biography. 7. Rockingham County (Va.)–History–19th century. 8. Rockingham
County (Va.)–Politics and government–19th century. 9. Shenandoah River Valley (Va. and W.
Va.)–History–Civil War, 1861–1865. 10. Mount Vernon Furnace (Rockingham County, Va.)–
History. I. Title.
  F232.R7F57 2012
  975.5'92203–dc23

2012020030

5 4 3 2 1

Contents

Preface

As the Civil War approached, one conviction put Samuel Hance Lewis on a collision course with his Secessionist neighbors in Virginia's Shenandoah Valley: he believed the United States should remain a single nation. George Washington's visit to the Lewis home was still within living memory, and principles of family members who helped found the nation remained paramount. Samuel Hance Lewis was convinced that the United States should hold together and sort out its problems under the Constitution. He taught his children to believe the same.

This Union Loyalist family formed part of what one historian terms "that small group of mid-nineteenth century southern whites who swam against the tide of public opinion, supported the Union and became staunch and consistent Republicans in the Reconstruction and post-Reconstruction eras."[1] The sagas of relatively few such Loyalists are chronicled. Indeed, they were long thought not worth remembering. After the war's end, it took nearly a century for emotions to cool to the point that Confederate partisans could begin distinguishing upstanding Union Loyalists from those native-born opportunists who sought personal gain.[2]

In the heat of wartime emotion, Union Loyalists differed in how they expressed their beliefs. Some said nothing, or plotted secretly. Others became intemperate and risked their lives. Most were harassed. Samuel Hance Lewis and his family sought to survive the war by taking a middle ground, "giving no cause of offence by overt act or anything of the sort." But neither did they hide their convictions, made clear even to Confederate Gen. Stonewall Jackson as he made their home his headquarters.

In living out this balancing act, the Lewis family, like some other fortunate Southern Loyalists, gained a measure of protection from its standing in the community. Samuel Hance Lewis built his home on ancestral land worked by slaves, rose to the rank of brigadier general in the Virginia militia, and was so strong an Episcopalian that he served on the board of the Virginia Theological Seminary for nearly a decade. The only clue that he might ever come to cross-purposes with neighbors was that he remained a steadfast Whig in a county dominated by Democrats—who, nevertheless, twice elected him to the state legislature. Three sons rose to prominence in his wake.

Lewis family members may have been in the political minority, but they held to their wartime views with sufficient discretion and lack of offensiveness that at two crucial points in Virginia's postwar history they could facilitate compromises that happened to place them in the majority, at the highest levels leadership.

Oldest son Charles Hance Lewis, trained as a lawyer, moved into the political world as a Whig newspaper editor and publisher. Near the end of the war he emerged as secretary of the commonwealth in the Unionists' alternative Restored Government of Virginia, based in Alexandria, and stayed in the post as that entity became the state government in Richmond. Cosmopolitan and able to express himself with ease, he later became U.S. minister resident to Portugal.

Second son John Francis Lewis found his calling in politics in 1861, when he was elected one of Rockingham County's three delegates to the secession convention in Richmond. When it came time to sign the ordinance of secession, he was the only delegate from east of the Allegheny Mountains who refused to sign. Through most of the war he was an owner of an iron furnace that employed and sheltered Union Loyalists. During political crises afterward, he was twice elected lieutenant governor and became one of Virginia's first two U.S. Senators seated at the end of Reconstruction. At one Republican national convention he was nominated for vice president.

As a teenager, youngest son Lunsford Lomax Lewis fled across the river with his family as Confederate Gen. Stonewall Jackson's culminating victory in his Shenandoah Valley campaign—the Battle of Port Republic—engulfed the family home. Two years later, he avoided conscription into the Confederate army by fleeing the valley altogether as a refugee under the protection of Union Gen. Philip Sheridan's army. After the war, he was secretary to Union Loyalist John Minor Botts, his father-in-law.

Though Republicans were considered by many to be un-Virginian, the Lewis family still so embraced and embodied the culture of the Old South that when a prominent politician publicly insulted his brother John, Lunsford Lewis followed the code of honor and challenged the offender to one of the last duels fought in the state. Lunsford Lewis became chief justice of Virginia's Supreme Court and in 1905 was the Republican candidate for governor. After his defeat, discouraged Republicans gave little challenge to Democrats until the civil rights era, when they retook the statehouse in the election of 1969.

This saga has fallen beneath general awareness not only because southern Union Loyalists were so long considered undeserving of serious attention, but also because no large archive of family papers survived to readily document the story. Its reconstruction has occurred over a long period and moved forward only under the most tenuous circumstances. It might have never evolved into book form at all were it not an inside job that provided unique access to family sources, for Samuel Hance Lewis was my great-great grandfather and his three prominent sons were my grandfather's uncles. Reassembling the pieces has been aided by my training in journalism, which, I trust, also inoculated me against the sentimental haze that too often shrouds the true picture of one's own family.

A dose of skepticism from a journalism background is helpful when dealing with testimonies by Union Loyalists before Southern Claims commissioners in the 1870s. They have made significant contributions to this book, particularly in reconstructing the story of Mount Vernon Furnace, the basis for the chapter titled "John F. Lewis's Private War." But such material must be treated carefully. Some accounts were, inevitably, elaborated or even invented to strengthen requests for personal compensation, and no one was in the hearing rooms to dispute them other than commissioners hearing the cases.

Overall, however, it is hard to believe that so many similar accounts of loyalties and experiences, made independently at different times by so many persons from far-flung areas, could have been entirely concocted and coordinated in advance of the testimonies. Importantly, a large number of observations were made in passing about other Loyalists and had no bearing on the claims of the individuals being heard. Such fragmentary comments, when pieced together, yield unexpected insights into aspects of wartime that are otherwise unrecorded.

"Professing nothing he did not believe, nor concealing his sentiments, at the same time giving no cause of offence by overt act or anything of the sort, he got through the trying period of the war, all things considered, pretty well."

—Lunsford Lomax Lewis,
writing of his father in *A Brief Narrative*, 1915

Samuel Hance Lewis of Lewiston

The springtime whites and purples of Virginia's dogwoods and rhododendrons had given way to the mountain laurels' pink, rioting in early summer as Lunsford Lomax Lewis, 14, made his way home westward over the Blue Ridge Mountains from boarding school in Albemarle County. Back in Rockingham County, he expected just another homecoming. But it was June 1861, and he found his older friends enlisting in a southern army. That sounded like a good idea. He told his father he wanted to sign up, too. He was hardly prepared for Samuel Hance Lewis's response.

"His reply was an indignant refusal to give his assent to allow his son to commit treason," Lunsford recalled years later. "[He] coupled his refusal with a threat to thrash me soundly if he heard me express any such desire again."

That said, the aging Samuel Hance Lewis calmed down a bit, and some of the emotion built up during the secession crisis while his son was away began to lift.

"He then for the first time explained to me the alleged causes of the war, and that on the Confederate side it was a wicked rebellion,"

Samuel Hance Lewis was a firm believer in the need to preserve the Union.

remembered Lunsford Lewis. "He explained to me what I never before knew anything of, namely the theory of the constitution of the United States. [He] pointed out the fact that it was made by the people of the United States, that it was the supreme law of the land and recognized no such right as secession.

"I abandoned all desire, thereupon, to go into the Confederate Army, and was throughout the war loyal to the government of the United States."[1]

Samuel Hance Lewis, born in 1794, seemed every inch the iconic southern country squire. Standing "six feet high, spare and well proportioned," his eyes blue, his hair light, his gait erect, he had a commanding presence that did not intimidate but made him "thoroughly approachable by all classes in the community." While he stressed traits of "industry, frugality and temperance" in raising his children, honesty was paramount. "I have never known a man," son Lunsford remarked, "who had less patience with a liar, or more contempt for one." When riding, he was certain to be on a good horse. He enjoyed following hounds on a fox hunt and angling for trout in mountain streams. He was a good shot and liked to initiate others, as he once put it, "into the tactics of a deer hunt."[2]

His background may seem identical to that of many traditional southerners advocating secession and armed rebellion. But some threads explain why he differed so strongly on one point with his mainstream countrymen, how he developed the inner compass enabling him to remain firm but diplomatic even as war swirled around him, and what made his example one that three sons successfully emulated, with far-reaching repercussions.

The death of his older brother Thomas in 1840, at 47, left Samuel Hance Lewis in the role of family patriarch and preserver of family traditions, one he filled with relish. As frontier historian Lyman Draper was gathering his noted collection of material in the 1840s, it was Samuel Hance Lewis who reported long-ago conversations with his elders that now provide the sole source of many details cited by historians. Another inquirer received a letter from Samuel Hance Lewis recounting a conversation he once held with an elderly general who had been an aide to George Washington at Valley Forge. Lewis contributed a history of the Revolutionary War–era Anglican Church in Rockingham County to Bishop William Meade's *Old Churches, Ministers, and Families of Virginia*.[3]

Most significantly for his family's role in the Civil War era, Samuel Hance Lewis intertwined his respect for the memory of his forebears with conviction of the wisdom of their political principles. These beliefs were so firmly ingrained, wrote Lunsford, that, "indeed, it may almost be said that with him they were hereditary." One defining tribal memory was of a great-grandfather who stood up to an Old World overlord, fled to the Virginia frontier, and founded a family committed to the American Revolution.[4]

The great-grandfather, John Lewis, 50, was inside his paternal farmstead in northern Ireland when the landlord, seeking to evict the Lewises, fired from horseback into the home, mortally wounding John Lewis's bedridden brother and striking his wife, Margaret Lynn Lewis, in the hand. John Lewis, enraged, seized his shillelagh, rushed outside and struck the assailant, who fell from his horse, dead. John Lewis fled to America. His family followed, and in the early 1730s they found safety deep in Virginia's Shenandoah Valley among the earliest settlers in what became Augusta County. John Lewis prospered, as did his four sons.[5]

Thomas, the eldest, was named county surveyor when Augusta County was organized in 1745 and supervised street planning for its county seat,

A line of trees through the center of this vista, looking west in about 1900, marks the course of the Shenandoah River. On the near side of the river at right are the Lynnwood home and outbuildings on the site of Thomas Lewis's 1750s home. To the right is the southern end of Massanutten Mountain. At far left center is the Lewis mill. Across the river from the mill is the site of the Gabriel Jones home.

Staunton. His journal of an expedition in the wilderness for Lord Fairfax with fellow surveyor Peter Jefferson, father of the future president, has been termed "a minor classic of American exploration." Thomas Lewis in 1749 married Jane Strother, born near Fredericksburg, where the Strothers had settled after their voyage from England in 1650. Two of his fellow county officials married Jane's sisters. From Staunton the three young families moved some twenty miles northeast to fertile lowlands where the North and South rivers join to form the South Fork of the Shenandoah. A quarter century later that area became the southern corner of the new Rockingham County.[6]

Elements that would shape the region's appearance at the time of the Civil War began falling into place. Jane Strother Lewis's sister Agatha was the bride of John Madison, Augusta County clerk. They built their home at what became the western edge of the village of Port Republic. Three miles to the east, Margaret and her husband, Gabriel Jones, the irascible county attorney, built on the edge of their 1,200 acres above the northern bank of the Shenandoah. Thomas and Jane Lewis settled across the Shenandoah on its southern bank, on 2,000 acres ranging from the river plain into the densely wooded foothills of the Blue Ridge. In surveying his new property, Thomas Lewis identified a barely perceptible rise not far from the river that sometimes becomes an island during the river's flooding. There he built his home.

Thomas Lewis, too near-sighted for military service, gathered a library of unusual size for the frontier. He was a delegate to county and state con-

Lynnwood, shown in about 1910, was built by in 1814 Charles Lewis on or near the site of the home his father built near the Shenandoah River.

ventions supporting the American Revolution, and in 1776 was elected to Virginia's first House of Delegates under the new state constitution. In 1788, two years before his death, Thomas Lewis and his brother-in-law and neighbor Gabriel Jones were Rockingham County's delegates to the Virginia convention considering the proposed U.S. Constitution. Their strong Federalist convictions and those of most delegates from the Shenandoah Valley and the Tidewater added votes to help future president James Madison's efforts to override the anti-Federalists. By a vote of 89 to 79, Virginia became the tenth state to ratify the constitution.[7]

Thomas Lewis left his estate only to his two youngest sons, Charles, then 17, and Benjamin, 11, with strict moral requirements: "that Neither of them take to those Detestable Vices of Immoderate Drinking Gaming or Gambling the certain ruin of those who follow such Practices . . . and live Soberly honestly & Chastly & Shun those Rocks their unhappy Brothers have Split upon." Charles received the eastern part of the estate, including the family home. Benjamin inherited the western portion. "They were very social, well informed, respectable gentleman," recounted a nephew, George Rockingham Gilmer, later governor of Georgia, who first visited his uncles in 1808.[8]

Benjamin Lewis was one of five trustees of the new village of Port Republic. The large frame home he built—Westwood—was sold after his death in 1830. His three children and their families left with their widowed mother for a swath of central Missouri that attracted so many settlers from Virginia that it was known as Little Dixie.[9]

Charles Lewis remained on the family land. In 1792 he had married Anne Hance, from the western shore of Chesapeake Bay in Maryland's Calvert County, where the tobacco-growing Hance family had arrived from England in 1659.[10] As Revolutionary-era hostility toward anything English faded, Charles Lewis helped revive Rockingham County's ties with the Episcopal Church. The local Anglican tradition had begun with the three Strother sisters from eastern Virginia, where their forebears had brought it from England. In 1785 John and Agatha Strother Madison's son James Madison—second cousin of the future president and Charles Lewis's first cousin—became Virginia's first resident Episcopal bishop. Charles Lewis was such a loyal Episcopalian that, thought Bishop William Meade, "a truer friend to the Church, when friends were few, a more perfect gentleman, and a worthier citizen, could not be found."[11]

Charles Lewis studied at Liberty Hall, where his father had been a trustee when it was named Augusta Academy. He sent his three sons to its successors, Washington Academy and Washington College—ultimately Washington and Lee University—at Lexington. In March 1814, at the site of his parents' home he completed a two-and-a-half-story brick Federalist-style residence that became known as Lynnwood, after the maiden name of his paternal grandmother, Margaret Lynn Lewis. At a time when a wide selection of commodities was hard to find locally, the family formed a cooperative named Chambers & Lewis, run by sons Samuel Hance and Charles Jr. and Mustoe Chambers—who was married to their sister Mary Anne—that purchased supplies in quantity from distant sources. This freed Charles Lewis and his eldest son, Thomas, to attend to business and financial affairs in Richmond, Alexandria, and Warm Springs, where cousins were developing curative spas.[12]

Slaves were part of the picture, though not precisely in the manner of the rest of the South. Shenandoah Valley farms lacked the hundreds of African American slaves common on the largest Tidewater plantations, though one of every five valley inhabitants was a slave. There was also less class distinction and a less rigid hierarchy of labor; valley farmers often worked side by side with their slaves and during peak seasons hired them out to neighboring farmers. In 1788 Thomas Lewis ran his 2,000 acres with only eight slaves—and he was the third largest slaveholder in Rockingham County, the largest having twelve. As one measure of how productivity was increasing, in 1810 Charles and Benjamin Lewis had forty-nine slaves on the same lands—Charles had twenty-six and his brother twenty-three—tying with the number of the largest slaveholder in the county. Many farmers, however, had none. With soil and climate ideal for growing wheat, Rockingham County was in the heart of Virginia's primary wheat-growing region. Cash crops could bring prosperity to lone farmers owning as few as 200 acres. But to meet the grow-

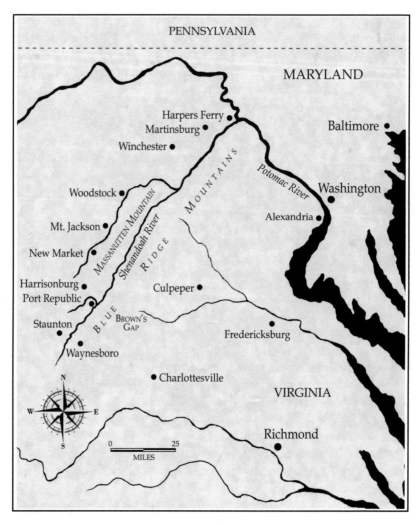

Virginia's Shenandoah Valley extends northeastward west of the Blue Ridge, Mountains, and is briefly divided by the Massanutten Mountain range.

ing demand from the East for flour, farmers had to build wagons and do the hauling themselves. For Rockingham County growers, the difficult route over the mountains to Richmond could take two weeks.[13]

Navigating boatloads of flour down the Shenandoah River to Harpers Ferry and on to the Potomac was an obvious alternative, if the rocky channel could be cleared and widened. That became a goal of the Potomac Company, established in 1785 and headed by George Washington. The future president had discussed just such a project with Thomas Lewis the previous fall, during a two-night visit to the Lewis home. But the Potomac Company never got beyond opening, in 1807, the river's lowest forty miles to navigation. A group of area residents decided they could complete the work themselves for little more than the Potomac Company had paid its engineers. In 1813 they organized the New Shenandoah Company to make the river navigable downstream from Port Republic to Harpers Ferry.[14]

President of the new company was Charles A. Stuart, state senator from Augusta County and a grandson of Thomas Lewis. Directors were Stuart's uncle Charles Lewis, David Galladay of Augusta County, and John Gatewood of Shenandoah County. The three directors became the contractors. They borrowed $85,000—$1.5 million in present dollars. Despite their lack of experience in such an undertaking, by 1824 they managed to finish clearing the South Fork of the Shenandoah from Port Republic to the Potomac. Put in place were 360 small dams and other works that raised the water level for cumbersome flatboat freighters known as gundalows. Though its population hardly grew beyond 200, Port Republic boomed as a commercial and industrial center, with boat yards, well-stocked stores, mills, tanneries, churches, and taverns. Charles Lewis built a gristmill beside the Shenandoah 200 yards west of his home, at what was known as Lewis Ford, and took advantage of the new access to markets.[15]

Despite his social and business standing, for most of his life Charles Lewis was a political throwback. He held to his father's Federalist Party even as it was collapsing nationally and as newcomers—most of them Republicans, as Democratic-Republicans were called—raised the number of citizens of German origin to 75 percent of Rockingham County's population. Charles Lewis was named justice of the peace as a Federalist and, in 1812, was elected county sheriff. But after that, as nephew George Rockingham Gilmer observed, Charles Lewis and his brother Benjamin "were excluded from office by their being Federalists, when almost all others in Rockingham were Republicans." By the time of his death in 1832, Charles Lewis had followed former Federalists into the Whig Party. Whigs, on the front line of the emerging market economy, championed a tariff to protect industries, public funding of internal improvements, and general economic development, while Democrats, generally agrarians, favored free trade and more gradual growth.[16]

Charles Lewis's son Samuel Hance Lewis embraced the Federalist-Whig political tradition. After attending Washington College, he went on to study law in Staunton in the office of Chapman Johnson, then serving in the state senate and later a leading lawyer in Richmond. But rather than practice law he focused on farming. Knowing that his older brother, Thomas, would inherit Lynnwood, Samuel took his inheritance early in family acreage to the south,

The Lewis Family

Children of **Charles Lewis** (1772–1832) and Anne Hance (ca. 1775–1840)

Thomas Lewis (1792–1840)
m. Delia Mildred Fletcher (1814–60)

Samuel Hance Lewis (1794–1869)
m. (1) Nancy Cameron Lewis (1795–1841)

> **Charles Hance Lewis** (1816–80)
> m. Ellen Tayloe Lomax (1811–1851)
>
> **John Francis Lewis** (1818–95)
> m. Serena Helen Sheffey (1823–1901)
>
> **Samuel Hance Lewis Jr.** (1819–92)
> m. Louisiana Sappington Dabney (1834–1907)
>
> **Harriet Anne Lewis** (1821–22)
>
> **Elizabeth Rachel Lewis** (1823–97)
> m. James Clifton Wheat (1812–1902)
>
> **Mary Lewis** (1825–70)
>
> **Nancy Lewis** (1827–27)
>
> **Anne Lewis** (1829–51)
>
> **Margaret Lynn Lewis** (1832–88)
>
> **William Meade Lewis** (1835–78)

m. (2) Anna Maria Lomax (1808–53)

> **Charlotte Thornton Lewis** (1844–1937)
> m. Beverley Blair Botts (1830–97)
>
> **Lunsford Lomax Lewis** (1846–1920)
> m. (1) Rosalie Summers Botts (1836–78)
> m. (2) Janie Looney (1851–1940)
>
> **Cornelia Juliet Lewis** (1847–71)
>
> **Anna Maria Lewis** (1851–1938)
> m. Charles Maurice Hall Smith (1851–1903)

m. (3) Martha E. Jones Fry (1807–70)

Charles Lewis Jr. (1796–1877)
m. Nancy F. Allen (1802–65)

Mary Anne Lewis (1797–1880)
m. Mustoe Chambers (1790–1865)

Elizabeth Mackall Lewis (1799–1801)

Gabriel Jones Lewis (1801–02)

Margaret Strother Lewis (1803–89)
m. Charles B. Tippett (1801–67)

stretching from the edge of the river plain into the wooded foothills of the Blue Ridge. On "a commanding eminence" a half mile south of his ancestral home, he hired builder Overton Gibson to put up the two-story brick Lewiston, finished in spring 1827. Typical of new larger homes in the Shenandoah Valley, it opened from a portico into a central hallway, with a large parlor on the left and a dining room on the right. There were twelve-foot ceilings downstairs and ten-foot ceilings upstairs. From the portico, the vista past Lynnwood focused six miles beyond on the sharp southern end of Massanutten Mountain, the slender ridge rising from the river plain to divide the lower Shenandoah Valley.[17]

Samuel Hance Lewis, 33, moved in with his wife, Nancy Cameron Lewis, 32—she was also his second cousin—and their five children, a sixth soon to arrive. After twenty-six years of marriage, Nancy died, in 1841, leaving four sons and four daughters. A year later Samuel married Anna Ma-

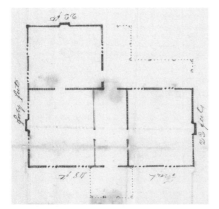

The builder's floor plan of Lewiston, completed in 1827, shows an entrance through a portico into a central hallway, flanked by two large rooms and opening at the rear onto a gallery beside an ell. The photo of Lewiston in about 1890 shows how closely this structure, rebuilt after a fire in 1875 with an extended ell, resembles the original home.

ria Lomax, 34, of Fredericksburg, second daughter of John Tayloe Lomax, a noted jurist and the first professor of law at the University of Virginia. But nearly eleven years later—in spring 1853—Anna Maria died after a lingering illness, leaving three daughters and a son. In 1856 Samuel married Martha Jones Fry, 49, a widow.[18]

By then the Lewiston property had grown to 750 acres, half woodland and the rest cultivated, much in corn and various types of wheat plus rye and tobacco. Samuel took special pride in his watermelons and his apple orchard. Near the gristmill, a sawmill cut timber into boards and fence rails. When winter froze a pond on a nearby hill, the ice was cut and stored in an insulated ice house.[19]

The mechanical reaper being developed by Cyrus McCormick of nearby Rockbridge County would eventually revolutionize farm operations. But in 1844 the Lewiston tobacco harvest alone took six days. Harvesting a local wheat crop could require more than a dozen hands; once grain ripened and before it could be spoiled by bad weather, men—often slaves—had to cut the stalks with hand-swung cradle scythes while others raked it and bound the sheaves into shocks to dry. Three handwritten pages at the back of the Lewiston Bible, printed in 1833, list a "Record of Servants" beginning with six—Jim, Bob, Jacob, Lucy, Charles, and Jack, all between the ages of 18 and 62. Their names are followed by dates of birth, and sometimes death, of children. Bob and Lucy's first child was Abram James, born in 1819. Of Samuel Hance Lewis, James recalled that as a slave he "was born near his estate, was purchased by him before I can recollect and I lived with him several years after the war. I remained with the family up to the death of my old master.[20]

For Samuel Hance Lewis's view on slavery we have only this statement from his son Lunsford, a judge whose candor in other accounts of family matters suggests he followed his father's mandate for telling the truth: "As for slavery, while he owned slaves, he, like many Virginians, considered the institution an evil, and he rejoiced when it ceased to exist." Samuel's close friend Bishop William Meade took the unusual step for a southern Episcopal clergyman of speaking out strongly against slavery, whether or not, as the majority of southern clergymen of all denominations believed, slavery was sanctioned in the Bible.[21]

Bishop Meade's primary mission was the evangelism of western Virginia. The Episcopal Church was beginning to recover from effects of the anticlerical emotions of the Great Awakening and of the anti-British mood that tarred Episcopalians with the same brush as the Church of England, from which Episcopalians separated after the Revolution. Meade could count on the Lewises, part of "a faithful remnant of old Virginia families devoted to the liturgy of the Book of Common Prayer." Samuel Hance Lewis had supported the church since his mid-20s, when he donated toward the monthly preaching in Port Republic by the rector of Staunton's Trinity Church. In May 1822 he forded the river to call on his great-aunt Margaret Strother Jones—alert and active five months before her death at 96—and received a donation of $10 for the Rockingham Bible Society.[22]

At Lewiston, as early as 1833 Samuel was hosting Bishop Meade, who would spend the night before preaching the next morning in Port Republic, Harrisonburg, or Staunton. Four years later Samuel did his part for evangelism by helping organize the Staunton church's satellite chapel at Folly Mills, fifteen miles southwest of Port Republic, as the independent Boyden Parish. It would struggle, with never more than two dozen members. He was a frequent delegate to diocesan and national church conventions. For at least seven years, through 1850, he was a trustee of Alexandria's Virginia Theological Seminary, chaired by Bishop Meade. In 1856 Diocesan Finance Chairman Samuel Hance Lewis and five of his fellow committee members personally advanced $2,389, the present-day equivalent of more than $60,000, to keep Virginia Female Institute—now Stuart Hall School—from being sold for its debts.[23]

Samuel Hance Lewis also ranged beyond Lewiston as he rose through the ranks of the Virginia Militia, organized to defend against domestic disorder and foreign invasion and providing good business and social networking. In 1815 he was a captain of artillery in Rockingham County's regiment. Three years later he was reimbursed five dollars "for musick employed at 2 company musters, to wit a drummer and fifer." The scene was no doubt like a reported muster of neighboring Augusta County's Staunton Light Infantry: a formation of colonels, majors, and captains wearing brass-buttoned "coats of ancient pattern" of dark blue cloth, with long swallowtails and shining epaulets—all enhanced, in later years, by plumed cocked hats and red sashes. As the leaders marched forward, ranks of rifle-bearing privates in hunting shirts fell in. "An admiring crowd followed the company wherever it went."[24]

By 1822 Samuel Hance Lewis, 28, had been promoted to colonel. In 1837 both houses of Virginia's general assembly approved his promotion as the Seventh Brigade's brigadier general, a rank he was known by for the rest of his life. It was no honorific appointment. In the 1840s, the general of the Seventh Brigade had to manage an average of 8,000 militiamen from five counties and divided into eleven regiments.[25]

Politically, Gen. Samuel Hance Lewis overcame the handicap of being a Whig party activist and enthusiastic supporter of Henry Clay in a strongly Democratic county. Though Lunsford thought his father "not in any way a politician," he had sufficient personal popularity to be elected to public office.

In 1824 he ran for one of the county's two seats in the House of Delegates, and of five candidates came in a distant fifth. But two years later he was successful. He was elected to two terms, serving in Richmond in 1827 and 1828. He was presiding county judge for several decades and county sheriff in 1847–48. He continued his father's interest in Shenandoah River navigation as treasurer of the New Shenandoah Company.[26]

One Whig tenet resonating with Samuel Hance Lewis was temperance. Nearly four decades before, the vice of "immoderate drinking" had helped cause three of his uncles to be disinherited. Whigs believed effects of strong drink produced by unregulated distilleries were dangerously sapping the young nation's energies. The American Temperance Society was formed in 1826 and in three years had more than 1,000 individual societies—fifty-two of them in Virginia—and boasted solid achievements.[27]

In September 1835 Samuel Hance Lewis displayed his strong moral imperative and gift of rhetoric in remarks before a Harrisonburg convention of Rockingham County temperance societies. "We owe it to ourselves, our families, our friends & neighbors, our Country, above all to God" to address the issue, he declared. "The pernicious fluid which has filled the world with war is daily sending its thousands to the regions of despair" and wasting "enormous sums of money which the people are compelled to contribute for the support of the paupers, the confinement of the lunatics & the punishment of the criminals it has made." Whatever the cause of the victim's unhappiness, "he flies to the bottle to drown his unavailing sorrow. . . . The remedy does but aggravate in a thousand fold the disease—guilt & degradation and despair added to grief—and then comes remorse, like the fabled vultures of Prometheus, to prey upon his vitals, until he sinks into a premature grave." Saloons abetted the problem, he said, in a concise phrase ideal for a sound bite in a latter-day media age: "I cannot look upon a tippling house in any other light than as a nursery of drunkards."[28]

In public addresses on another subject, Samuel Hance Lewis spoke on the nation's founding principles at Washington's Birthday celebrations and other gatherings. He had special admiration for Alexander Hamilton, whom he thought "the most brilliant American statesman." He was a friend and admirer of fellow Virginian John Marshall, longtime chief justice of the U.S. Supreme Court.

But it was the achievement of nationhood that he held dearest. In the final analysis, said son Lunsford, "he was a Virginian, and he loved Virginia, but the Union, which he deemed essential as well to Virginia as to her sister States, was his country."[29]

2

No to Secession

Should slavery be extended into the nation's western territories? And if so, how? Presidential candidates in 1860 reflected a national geographical split over the incendiary questions. Abraham Lincoln of Illinois, candidate of the northern Republican Party, would bar any extension of slavery. Democrats broke apart over the issue. The candidate of Northern Democrats, Stephen A. Douglas of Illinois, would allow territorial residents to decide for themselves. The candidate of Southern Democrats, John C. Breckinridge of Kentucky, would not restrict slavery in the territories at all.

A fourth presidential candidate, Tennessee's John Bell of the new Constitutional Union Party, subordinated that question and threats of secession to what his party believed to be the overarching issue at stake, articulated in a simple two-paragraph platform emphasizing support for "the Constitution, the Union and the Laws."

The Constitutional Union Party found its greatest support in border states, especially among men like Samuel Hance Lewis, who believed that it went "without saying" that any issue that would sunder the United States was "repugnant." For him, as with so many slaveholding Union Loyalists throughout the South, slavery could not be allowed to destroy the nation, any self-interest in the institution aside. In 1860 Samuel had eleven adult slaves and nine younger ones, son John F. had four adult slaves and four children, and Samuel Jr. had a family of four, including two children. But that was immaterial. "The adoption of the Constitution had saved the Union from anarchy," Samuel believed, and "to destroy the Union would be an unspeakable calamity." Citizens indeed had an "inherent right of revolution." But that was "a very different thing from the right of a State in her sovereign capacity to withdraw from the Union."[1]

Samuel Hance Lewis's oldest son Charles Hance Lewis, 44, had been warning of the dangers of states seceding over any such disagreement for a decade and a half, since his days as a newspaper editor. In early 1860 he was elected an alternate delegate to the national Constitutional Union Party convention in Baltimore. A year later second son John Francis Lewis, 42, was a delegate to a Virginia convention that would actually vote on secession. Like their father, both men held the same beliefs through careers that varied little from those of peers who wound up on the opposite end of the political spectrum.

Charles H. Lewis had followed in his father's footsteps by getting a "good education" and reading law in Staunton, except that, unlike his father, he continued in the legal profession. He was admitted to the bar and began to practice law, his office on the east side of Staunton's courthouse square. At age 24 he married Ellen Tayloe Lomax of Fredericksburg, age 29, fourth daughter of the jurist John Tayloe Lomax. In the 1840s Charles served on his father's general staff in the state militia as brigade inspector, with the rank of major. He involved himself in the cause of public education as president of Staunton's Educational Association in 1846, when criticism of Virginia's lack of a strong system of public schools was rising.[2]

In the course of all this, Charles H. Lewis developed a talent for writing poetry, so much in vogue nationwide that many newspapers published a poem on the front page of each edition. When an issue arrived in the *Rockingham Register*'s office of the Richmond-based *Southern Literary Messenger*—lately edited by Edgar Allan Poe—the arrival in itself could merit mention in the newspaper. One *Messenger* listing of its contributing "prose and poetical writers" ranged from Henry Wadsworth Longfellow to John Quincy Adams to Charles Hance Lewis. In September 1842 the *Messenger* published a stylishly sentimental poem by Charles H. Lewis titled "Away from the Haunts of Men," described by its author as "lines suggested by a visit to Crab Bottom, Pendleton Co., Va." For its front page the *Staunton Spectator* once picked up his poem "Before This Head Was Gray" that had been published in another leading literary journal, New York's *The New World*.[3]

Not all of his associates were impressed. Staunton attorney and former state senator John Howe Peyton thought him in a local "nest of singing birds of which he has always been a warbler of the first feather." Peyton believed he should "give up on poetry and enter on practical life. Poetry is too unprofitable for a man working for his daily bread." Peyton's son John Lewis Peyton, Charles H. Lewis's third cousin and a writer of less poetic bent, offered a backhanded compliment: "Though his fugitive pieces abounded in defects of execution and exhibited evident marks of haste, they also exhibited beauties of no ordinary kind."[4]

Whether prompted by such ridicule, by the sense of more appealing opportunities elsewhere, or by some sort of marital discord, at the age of 30 Charles H. Lewis made an abrupt turn. His wife took their two young children and went home to her parents in Fredericksburg. In January 1847 he put their house up for sale, turned over his law practice to fellow attorney and militia officer John B. Watts and set off ninety miles down the valley to Martinsburg in Berkeley County, where he had just purchased the *Martinsburg Gazette*. He assured clients he would return for the May term of the Augusta County court to attend to any unfinished business.[5]

As a newspaper owner, editor, and publisher, Charles H. Lewis could use his writing ability and be paid for it, though he would be concentrating on public issues and not poetry. In March 1847 he pledged readers "to exercise the most watchful care that nothing shall appear in the columns of the *Gazette* calculated to prejudice the cause of virtue and sound morality." He promised that, "as a Virginian by birth and education, and devotedly attached to my native soil," he would strongly advocate "a liberal yet judicious system of Internal Improvements and a plan of Common School Education, which will place the means of acquiring useful knowledge within the reach of all."[6]

As for the emerging doctrine of states' rights, he declared: "I am a Whig . . . because I regard the great body of the Whig party as being diametrically opposed to those radical and distinctive principles, so alarmingly prevalent in some of the States of our confederacy, and which threaten, at no distant day, to destroy the fair fabric of our Union." The nameplate atop the front page previously offered a rambling mission statement: "A Family Newspaper Devoted to General Intelligence, Advertising, Politics, Literature, Arts and Science, Agriculture &c." Charles H. Lewis changed that to match only a basic principle of the Whig party: "We stand upon the broad platform of the Constitution." He hired a new pressman, who improved the typography, and sprinkled a few of his own works among the weekly poems on the front page.

He added a dash of poetic euphoria to his report of venerated Whig senator Henry Clay's visit to Martinsburg in January 1848: "Hundreds of patriot bosoms heaved with emotions of enthusiasm never felt before." Ten months later Berkeley County produced a rare Whig majority in a presidential election, for Zachary Taylor and Millard Fillmore. An exultant follow-up meeting of the county's Whig executive committee—Charles H. Lewis was a member—closed with "three deafening cheers for Taylor and Fillmore."[7]

Charles H. Lewis ran the *Martinsburg Gazette* for just over two years, until fall 1849. The 1850 census shows him as an editor living in a hotel in nearby Moorefield in Hardy County, where he may have been associated with the new *Hardy Whig*, though his name cannot be found in surviving fragmentary details about the paper. Whig newspapers, however, were losing their base of support as the party disintegrated over the issue of extending slavery into the territories. In Virginia some Whigs joined with remnants of the Know-Nothing Party to become the American Party. Charles H. Lewis soon appeared in Richmond, where in 1855 he began editing the new *Semi-Weekly American* with his friend Tyre Maupin, former editor of the *Harrisonburg Republican* and member of a Whig family in Port Republic. In early 1857 he was putting out the *American* with an associate named Edward W. Perry.[8]

But the short-lived American Party was already in decline. Charles H. Lewis gave up on publishing, went back to Lewiston, and hung out his shingle as a lawyer once again. He continued in the Virginia Militia as a colonel. At July Fourth ceremonies in Harrisonburg's courthouse square in 1860, the *Rockingham Register* reported, he presented a flag purchased by "ladies of the town" to a formation of the Rockingham Rifles and made "a very beautiful and appropriate speech full of stirring thoughts." Given *Register* editor John H. Wartman's states' rights leanings, those "stirring thoughts" could have gone unreported for being pro-Union, for Charles H. Lewis was not hiding his opinions. Earlier in the year he praised fellow attorney and local congressman John T. Harris for favoring the Union and advised him: "The excitement gotten up by a few madcaps and disunionsts at Harrisonburg has provoked a very strong reactionary feeling in the county, and you need not be surprised to hear of a thundering Union meeting before long."[9]

Charles H. Lewis became active in the American Party's short-lived successor, known simply as the Opposition Party. In the South it was "a haven for Whigs isolated from the Democratic Party and repelled by the Republican Party's sectional and radical nature."[10] In Virginia, an Opposition Party convention in Richmond in March 1860 chose Charles H. Lewis as a senatorial elector from Rockingham and Pendleton counties and picked him to attend the emerging Constitutional Union Party's upcoming convention in Baltimore as his district's alternate to delegate Alexander H. H. Stuart, a prominent Unionist from Staunton. Virginians William C. Rives of Albemarle County and John Minor Botts of Richmond were among candidates for the Constitutional Union presidential nomination. On the second ballot, however, former Whig senator John Bell of Tennessee was nominated for president and former Massachusetts governor Edward Everett for vice president.[11]

In the presidential election of 1860, the Constitutional Union Party narrowly carried Virginia and also won the border states of Kentucky and Tennessee. Southern Democrat John C. Breckinridge—still James Buchanan's vice president—swept the Lower South. Northern Democrat Stephen A. Douglas carried only Missouri. Republican Abraham Lincoln won seventeen northern states and the election.

In Virginia, Bell had done particularly well in the eastern cities and in the Shenandoah Valley, and in other areas where Whigs had been strong. Breckinridge fared well among rural Democrats. Douglas's best areas were in some cities and a few onetime Whig strongholds. One of the half dozen counties he carried was Rockingham, where he was backed by the *Rockingham Register*.

The paper cut Lincoln little slack; it thought Douglas represented "the only hope of preserving, outside of an appeal to arms, the executive seat of the Government from being defiled and polluted by the contaminating stench of a Black Republican President." Despite such an outburst, the *Register* had no trouble proclaiming that restraint in making acid assessments was a virtue; when Douglas stopped in Harrisonburg on a swing through the Shenandoah Valley, the paper thought him "calm, sober, temperate." More than three-fourths of Rockingham voters supported the two candidates who opposed secession, Douglas and Bell, and clearly preferred that the nation stay together. But as the anti-Lincoln venom of the *Rockingham Register* foretold, Lincoln's national victory assured conflict. The next month South Carolina voted to secede from the Union. The six other states of the Lower South soon followed.[12]

The rash of secessions increased pressure on Gov. John Letcher to call Virginia's General Assembly to meet and discuss secession, still not a foregone conclusion in the state. The assembly gathered on January 7, 1861. Twelve days later it authorized election of delegates to a special Richmond convention to consider secession, while a separate ballot item would determine whether another general election should be called to vote on the convention's decision. The delegate election was set for February 4, which happened to be the same day seceded states of the Lower South formed their own government in Montgomery, Alabama. Despite Charles H. Lewis's political credentials and experience, Rockingham Unionists urged his well-liked younger brother, John F. Lewis, attractive as a political neophyte with as yet few opponents, to run for one of Rockingham County's three delegate slots.

For later biographies, John F. Lewis, born in 1818, reported his educational background as "at the old field school." The impression that he did not get beyond a small schoolhouse seems correct. Samuel Bassett French, who in the nineteenth century compiled biographical sketches of nearly 9,000 Virginians, obtained anecdotal information from his subjects' family members and set it down. In the case of John F. Lewis, he wrote: "His education was limited. He was too full of fun and frolic, so his father put him to work on his farm until he was fourteen years of age."[13]

The son proved so capable that, according to French, he took over general management of Lewiston in his father's absence. In 1842 John married Serena Helen Sheffey, daughter of the late Daniel Sheffey, a four-term Federalist congressman from Staunton a few decades before. They began raising the first of their seven children in a home on his family's lands. His duties expanded to include running the family's gristmill and shepherding its products to market down the river, which required quick reactions, physical strength, and a streak of independence. On one occasion in fall 1846, John F. Lewis, 28, and legendary riverboat captain Zachariah Raines were taking a dozen flat-bottomed boats laden with sacks of flour down the Shenandoah when they encountered a mill dam impassable by their heavily loaded boats. It took two grueling days to unload the flour onto wagons, haul the flour around the dam, and reload the cargo. Then they could continue their voyage to Harpers Ferry and down the Potomac to the port of Georgetown, in the District of Columbia.[14]

Through all this, John F. Lewis gained many friendships in Rockingham County and developed a clarity of thought, an ability to express himself, and a grasp of political concepts that suggest an educational level far beyond an "old field school." In the mid-1850s he reflected his father's social conscience as a member of the Port Republic Lodge of the Sons of Temperance. As political dissension increased, he held to his lifelong Whig beliefs by speaking in favor of the 1860 Constitutional Union Party candidates.[15]

Just before the filing deadline for candidates to the secession convention, John F. Lewis was convinced to run. He announced his candidacy in the newspaper, with the last of the eight other candidates,

As a young man, John F. Lewis helped manage the family's Lewiston property and mill and gradually became active in politics.

on January 25. It would be a short campaign; the election was only ten days away, and the convention was to begin in Richmond ten days after that, on February 13. He wasted no time in making it clear where he stood. "From every 'stump,' and by every other practicable means," wrote Lunsford Lewis, "my brother made clear to the people just what his position was. He declared himself unqualifiedly for the Union, and that if elected to the convention, under no circumstances would he vote for an ordinance of secession."[16]

John F. Lewis based his stand on the Constitution, "adopted by the people and therefore unable to be dissolved except by the action of the people in their sovereign capacity," as he put it. Therefore, "I do not believe in the right of secession. The concurrence of two-thirds of the States is required to alter or amend the Constitution. It is absurd, then, to contend that one can annul or destroy the whole. . . . I am determinedly opposed to trusting the final decision of the important and momentous question of the secession of Virginia from the Union to any Convention."[17]

Rockingham Register editor John Wartman took that with a grain of salt, supposing that all leading candidates may be "representatives of the strong Union sentiment of the county" but that, should "all just and proper efforts in that direction fail, then they will go, as Virginians and as Southern men, for the rights, the honor and the dignity of the old Commonwealth, out of the Union." One candidate, Dr. Samuel A. Coffman, had already suggested that was what he would do. Coffman promised to present a list of grievances "to the North, demand a full acquiescence or rejection, and if not accepted then I would secede, and not till then."[18]

John F. Lewis faced charges that he was "a Botts Whig and an abolitionist." Of those, he said, "to the first charge I plead guilty, the latter was too absurd to notice." He praised Northern Democrat Stephen A. Douglas, whom nearly half the county had voted for three months before, and Rockingham congressman John T. Harris, an independent Democrat whom the Lewises had not voted for in the last election. But he had no good words for the sectionalism of former Southern Democratic candidate John C. Breckinridge.[19]

Three of the nine convention candidates withdrew from the election a week before balloting. Among the remaining six, results were decisive. Unionists Samuel A. Coffman received 2,588 votes; John F. Lewis, 2,081; and Algernon Sidney Gray, 1,999, nearly twice as many as the candidate in fourth place. Banished to last place, with 503 votes, was Jacob N. Liggett, who had fumed: "I am violently opposed to the usurpative powers and tyrannical principles claimed and exercised by the Black Republican party, which from a small and insignificant band of traitors, despised and ridiculed even at the North, has grown to such great proportions as to elect a representative member to the highest office in the gift of the people of the United States."[20]

While Coffman and Gray ran as Democrats, John F. Lewis ran as a Whig, a moribund party still holding a southeastern Rockingham bastion so strong, the Democratic *Rockingham Register* complained, that Port Republic had become the county's "Gibraltar of Whiggery." Although a Whig presence also remained in other areas of Virginia, the party was so far gone nationally that when John F. Lewis was chosen, the astonished editor of the conservative *Baltimore American* thought a Whig's election to be "little short of a miracle." The *American* added of Rockingham's victorious Unionist delegates, with no little optimism: "Such facts speak trumpet-tongued the deep devotion of the people of Virginia to the Government which was established by the wisdom and consecrated by the best blood of their fathers."[21]

The *Register*'s John Wartman managed to control himself, blending in a back-handed dash of civility and charm to lighten the sting. "We were not one of those who voted for John F. Lewis for a seat in the Convention," he admitted, "but we feel free to say, from intimate acquaintance with him, that the good old Democratic county of Rockingham might and could have done a great deal worse than to elect him as one of her delegates. A more honest, high-minded and honorable gentleman than Jno. F. Lewis we have not the pleasure of knowing. His inveterate determined and pertinacious devotion to heterodox political notions, however, will not allow us to vote for him when we have intelligent and honorable gentlemen in the field who entertain correct political opinions."[22]

John F. Lewis chose to believe that since his Whig convictions had always been at odds with the county's heavily Democratic majority, his election did nothing less than reveal the county's absolute devotion to preserving the Union. "I am proud of old Rockingham's Union sentiments," he said. "What better evidence could she give of her devotion to the cause than the triumphant election of one who has all his life battled against her political principles."[23]

Indeed, election of a Whig opposed to secession along with election of two Democrats equally opposed did reflect Rockingham County's unity in opposing the measure a full three months after Lincoln's election. Another indicator is the county's vote on the other ballot item, on whether a statewide referendum would be required to ratify a convention decision to secede. Those favoring secession strongly opposed such a referendum, fearing that their purposes would not be served by getting too many people into the decision. Secession opponents strongly favored the vote as offering a backup means of defeating secession. The referendum item, approved statewide, passed in Rockingham County 2,489 to 589, reflecting the will of secession opponents by a margin of more than four to one.[24]

As the secession convention opened in the state capitol's Hall of the House of Delegates in Richmond on February 13, 1861, two-thirds of its delegates hoped to keep Virginia in the Union. The remaining third split into those who demanded secession—primarily from the heavily slaveholding eastern part of the state—and others, mainly from northwestern Virginia, who absolutely opposed it. If a way could be found for Virginia to stay in the Union, it appeared that the new Confederate government would be hard pressed to continue. If Virginia left and the seven other states of the Upper South followed, even Abraham Lincoln believed the Union had little chance of survival.[25]

John F. Lewis, rooming at Richmond's American Hotel with his fellow Rockingham delegates, was certain that secession would be defeated. "This Convention is determined not to secede for any cause that now exists or that is likely to arise," he wrote the *Register*, fulfilling a campaign promise to report regularly to its readers. "We are startled every day by reports intended to drive

John F. Lewis joined other delegates, two-thirds of them Unionists, as Virginia's Secession Convention opened at the state capitol in Richmond on February 13, 1861.

the convention to hasty actions," he told Congressman John T. Harris, "but I think there is backbone enough in the body to withstand the pressure." A large majority of the delegates, he calculated, had supported Constitutional Unionist John Bell for president. He sensed that the only bitterness at the convention early on was between former supporters of Douglas and Breckinridge. He dismissed *Register* editor John Wartman's efforts to unite Northern and Southern Democrats as fruitless: "Virginia is right, & we mean to stand by her & the Union as long as there is a shingle on the roof."[26]

Delegates, who moved to the Hall of the Mechanics' Institute and later back to the capitol, debated inconclusively for two months. Two weeks into the session a frustrated John F. Lewis was already complaining to *Register* readers that, "So far, we have done nothing." He admitted that "some of our men are weak in the back" and hedged his earlier no-secession assessment with, "Virginia will not secede unless her honor requires her to do so." But as he awaited a visit from brother Charles, he could still write home: "I am happy to think the disunion Whigs and the disunion Democrats are dead cocks in the pit."[27]

Indeed, Virginia Unionists, secure in their majority at the convention, felt little need for haste in the proceedings. They planned to complete a compromise resolution and adjourn in time for May elections. Unionists expected Secessionist candidates for the legislature would be soundly defeated, and that a mid-May peace conference among border states would then adopt a compromise to save the Union.[28]

As March wore on, John F. Lewis acknowledged that he had "received letters from [Rockingham] county saying mighty changes were going on in that part of the state, but I have noted one thing: none of the signatures affixed to the letters correspond with the names of any persons recorded on the poll book as having voted for me." He did suggest, "If I were certain that a majority of the people of Rockingham were in favor of secession, I would resign my place and let someone else be sent here." Otherwise, he swore, "Vote for secession I never will, and I will cut off my right arm rather than sign such an ordinance for no better cause than now exists, or is likely to exist."[29]

He did not make such comments, however, in formal debate. Two delegates elected as Unionists from neighboring Augusta County, John B. Baldwin and Alexander H. H. Stuart, are considered as being among the convention's three dozen most effective speakers. Rockingham's Algernon Gray made an emotional speech opposing secession. But John F. Lewis spoke not at all. "I am not a precipitator," he once explained. Nor, in his first elected position, was he enchanted with politics. Some unpleasant letters from back home aside, he found himself in the middle of a rift between John B. Baldwin and John Minor Botts over a meeting Baldwin had with Abraham Lincoln. And on the convention floor he had to deal with the likes of flamboyant former governor Henry A. Wise, who tried to wheedle him into changing sides. "This sort of life does not agree with me," he complained to his wife. "I never expect to be a candidate again, for any office," he wrote John T. Harris. "My desire is to represent my constituents faithfully in this convention, & then retire from the political world." Though a week later he made the point again—"I am tired of political life"—he would, in time, get over it.[30]

In pursuing their long-term agenda, Unionist delegates had been counting on the Lincoln administration's continued commitment to a peaceful solution of the crisis. But in early April they detected a shift in Washington toward military intervention. Some went to meet with the president and urge continued patience, though they returned to Richmond fearful. Even on April 12, when Confederate forces shelled Fort Sumter at Charleston, South Carolina, the convention majority remained hopeful that peace could be preserved. But three days later came the event that transformed convention debate: Lincoln's proclamation calling for 75,000 troops to quell the rebellion in the Lower South. Of those, 3,500 were to be from Virginia. With that, write William Freehling and Craig Simpson, it became clear to delegates that impending war "would force those on the fence to decide only one question: whom they most wished to kill. Most Virginians preferred to slay insulting Yankee coercers rather than erring Southern brothers."[31]

Debates over constitutional principles were suddenly eclipsed by the realization that there would be war, and that some of it would be fought in Virginia. More than three dozen delegates who had long opposed secession changed their minds. On April 17—two days after Lincoln's call for troops— delegates endorsed secession by a vote reported at 88 to 55. Most anti-secession votes came from northwestern Virginia, where discussion of separate statehood had already begun. But the vote was not binding unless approved by the statewide referendum, scheduled for May 23. Delegates adjourned to await results of that vote.[32]

Already, however, at the covert instigation of former governor Henry Wise, Virginia troops were seizing the federal arsenal at Harpers Ferry and the U.S. Navy Yard at Norfolk. Secession backers were not about to risk surrendering them just because some referendum might not approve their hard-won convention vote to secede. In Rockingham, as elsewhere, the civility evident two months before was suddenly in short supply. Public intimidation by secessionists "over-awed" even "the stoutest Union men." Voting in Virginia for more than a century had been by voice, so there were few secrets at the polls. Those arriving at the polls on May 23 in Rockingham County encountered threats "of hanging the first man to cast a Union vote." Some "talked about killing" John F. Lewis for his vote at the convention.[33]

John F. Lewis did not vote in the referendum; nor did his father, "realizing that the result was a foregone conclusion and that no good could be accomplished." One group of five Unionists did go to the polls at Port Republic late in the evening "to see how things were going." Finding hangers-on threatening anyone who might vote against secession, "we all came away and would not vote at all." In Harrisonburg, two brothers of convention delegate Algernon Gray stayed away until they found themselves visited by friends "who stated that our absence was exciting a good deal of attention and comment, of a threatening character, and that we would not be safe from the fury of the populace unless we voted. . . . We yielded, and just before sundown voted for the ratification."[34]

The convention's vote for secession was counted as ratified by 85 percent of Virginia voters. Approval was said to be 99 percent in Rockingham County, where votes against secession were recorded in only five of nineteen polling places. Twenty-two votes were reported as opposed out of the more than 3,000 cast. "3,000 Majority for Secession!!!" shouted a *Register* headline. "Make War for Rockingham!"[35]

Later estimates suggest that feelings of futility or fear of threats kept as many as 1,500 or more from voting. At Harrisonburg, official reports showed 621 in favor of secession and none opposed. At Port Republic, 105 were reported in favor and none opposed. Benjamin Haney, for one, had tried to vote against secession at Port Republic but fled to avoid being hanged and hid in a barn for several weeks. A few miles away, at Sparta, John Harrison did cast his vote against secession and was followed home, seized, threatened with death, and held prisoner for a day.[36]

Bowing to the majority, most valley delegates who had opposed secession joined others in returning to Richmond for the next session of the convention and began signing the ordinance at a formal ceremony on June 14. Opponents from northwestern Virginia did not bother going back, nor did John F. Lewis. When the last signature had been added to Virginia's Ordinance of Secession in December, only one delegate from east of the Allegheny Mountains remained who refused to sign. That one, true to his promise, was John F. Lewis.[37]

3

Cannon Fire Interrupts Breakfast

The misty southern headland of Massanutten Mountain rose knifelike six miles northward from Lewiston, across the South Fork of the Shenandoah River. Picturesque Massanutten may have been from the portico, but by creating a fifty-mile barrier through the lower Shenandoah Valley it provided the maneuvering challenge that soon turned the valley's Civil War campaigns into classics of military strategy and execution. Lewiston was in the way. It stood at the strategic intersection of what passed for a main road through the eastern section of the valley and of a network of twisting wagon roads up the western side of the Blue Ridge to Brown's Gap.

The Shenandoah Valley made both sides nervous. From Harpers Ferry, at the mouth of the Shenandoah River, a Confederate army could threaten Washington, D.C.—less than seventy miles away—or launch an invasion across the Potomac and the Maryland panhandle into Pennsylvania. Or Union troops could invade in the opposite direction, endangering one of the richest agricultural regions in the Confederacy. Either way, having an army tied up in the Shenandoah Valley could have a profound effect on the war to the east. The key point for controlling the valley was at Winchester, some fifteen miles beyond the northern end of Massanutten. During the war, Winchester would change hands incessantly, sometimes repeatedly during a single day.

When the Confederate capital moved from Montgomery, Alabama to Richmond, it faced the immediate threat of a Union army crossing south across the Potomac toward Richmond and also the risk of a Union invasion up the Shenandoah Valley to the west. On July 1, 1861, Virginia's pro-Union-turned-Confederate governor, John Letcher, was authorized to assign state militia units to temporary duty under Confederate control. Some units were rushed to northeastern Virginia to help face the Union army preparing to cross the Potomac. In Rockingham County, 800 militiamen were mobilized in the Fourth Regiment of Gen. Samuel Hance Lewis's old Seventh Brigade. They were dispatched north to protect Winchester. Reluctant conscripts included brothers Samuel H. Lewis Jr.—assigned as a captain and quartermaster—and Charles H. Lewis, made acting lieutenant colonel and adjutant to Col. William A. Maupin.[1]

"Believing that we would not hurt anybody, and that nobody would hurt us, I thought that it was best for us Union men to go into the militia," Charles H. Lewis later explained. He feared that their refusal to serve for what was anticipated as a brief period of enlistment might produce an issue that could jeopardize any possibility, however remote, that Virginia might still return to the Union.[2]

Three weeks later, at Manassas, Confederate forces routed the Union army that had crossed the Potomac. The heavy fighting ended hopes that the war would be quick and indicated the need for Virginia's militia troops to be merged into the Confederate Army for more effective organization and longer enlistment terms. As the process began in early September, Rockingham's Fourth Regiment was ordered home to be disbanded. On September 9 nearly 500 of the men reached Harrisonburg. Most had walked twenty miles that day from Mount Jackson and were "pretty well tired out and fagged down by the time they got within striking distance of home." But at ten the next morning they were ready to parade past the courthouse and stand in formation to hear Col. William Maupin's Regimental Order No. 35, read by Adjt. Col. Charles H. Lewis, thanking them for their service and disbanding the regiment.[3]

Having just turned 45, Charles H. Lewis was beyond military recruitment age. But his four younger brothers faced difficult choices.

John F. Lewis, 43, was already a prime target for southern partisans. For his unyielding pro-Union vote at the secession convention, "I was threatened repeatedly," he remembered. "They threatened to hang me several times, and I had some little apprehension at one time that they would do it." As he searched for a way to get through the war without directly serving the Confederacy, he knew that one of the region's major industries—Mount Vernon Furnace, its origins in an iron operation his mother's family began nearly a century earlier—had fallen on hard times. Virginia's sudden need for more iron improved the furnace's outlook, but it needed new management—which would be granted exemption from military duty. From running Lewiston and its mill, and navigating boat convoys down the river, John F. Lewis had the physical stamina to take on the strenuous work. He seized the unlikely opportunity. By the time the deal was done he had moved to a house near the furnace, four miles up in the mountains above Lewiston, with his wife and their five children. The oldest, Daniel Sheffey Lewis, 17, would also benefit from military exemption as an iron furnace worker.[4]

Samuel H. Lewis Jr., 41, soured on military service even before his regiment disbanded. "Conspicuous for his loyalty" to the Union and told that he and other militia men were about to be conscripted directly into the Confederate Army, he slipped away from the Winchester encampment and took a circuitous route back to his wife and young daughter at Riverside, their home

Samuel H. Lewis Jr., a reluctant state militia quartermaster captain in mid 1861, remained an outspoken Union Loyalist.

near the family mill on the Shenandoah. When enforcers came looking for deserters, he hurried up to the home of brother John. He later agreed to be detailed to area Confederate public works projects rather than having to serve in the army and also did civil service as a justice of the peace.[5]

William M. Lewis, 26 and single, and not inclined to be outspoken, followed the course of least resistance. The Confederacy would not have a conscription law for nine more months, but there were rumors that one was imminent. Rather than risk conscription and an unknown assignment, in June 1861 he enlisted in a local outfit, the 10th Virginia Infantry's Company B, known as the Rockingham Rifles. His first cousins James, Andrew, and George Lewis had already joined even though their father—William's uncle Charles Lewis Jr., 66—was still a Union Loyalist.[6]

Youngest brother Lunsford L. Lewis, 15, too young to face conscription, had yet to confront the issue.

The Union Army, stalled in its effort to seize Richmond, turned to invading the Shenandoah Valley in spring 1862. Union troops took Winchester and moved up the valley on both sides of Massanutten Mountain, intending to join at the far end and capture Confederate defenders in the vice. Union generals were dealing, however, with the pious and intense Thomas J. "Stonewall" Jackson, 38, a Mexican War veteran fresh from a decade of teaching at Virginia Military Institute and now in a gray uniform. Though outnumbered three to one, Jackson responded with a fast-moving campaign that dodged, unexpectedly struck, and generally outmaneuvered his foes, gaining him a reputation as one of the nation's most gifted military leaders. On March 23 he punched the Union army south of Winchester, at Kernstown, to get its attention and discourage it from leaving to reinforce federal troops near Richmond. With the Union army in pursuit, Jackson retreated along the western side of Massanutten, then swerved eastward into the Blue Ridge forests at Swift Run Gap, some fourteen miles northeast of Port Republic.

While sheltered from enemy attack, Jackson had to deal with an anti-conscription mutiny that has come to be known as the Rockingham Rebellion. An executive order incorporating remaining Virginia militia companies into

the Confederate Army brought particularly strong opposition from Rockingham County militiamen, a number of them pacifist German Baptist Brethren.
As many as 500 resisters sought refuge in the mountains nearby. An artillery
shelling and roundup of fugitives brought the matter to an end, signaling a
new hard line against civilian and military Confederate protestors.[7]

Among Jackson's key associates was his gifted topographer, Jedediah
Hotchkiss, who lived in Staunton and had a thorough knowledge of the region's terrain. At the end of April 1862, Hotchkiss took a brief leave home,
touched base with Confederate units facing Union troops camped around
Harrisonburg, and headed to Port Republic, where Union cavalry had been
reconnoitering.

On April 30 Hotchkiss stopped at Lewiston to feed his horse, then rode
on to climb the peak of Massanutten. He spent several hours observing movements of Union troops near Harrisonburg in the distance. At the end of the afternoon he reported back to Jackson, who had begun moving his troops down
from Swift Run Gap and southward along the river toward Port Republic.[8]

Hotchkiss and Jackson rode ahead to set up headquarters and spend
the night at Lewiston. There, Hotchkiss wrote, "We were quite hospitably
received." During pleasantries, Samuel Hance Lewis remarked that he was a
Union man "and expected to remain one." Jackson diplomatically replied that
he had also been a Union man but that after Lincoln's first call for troops Jackson and his host had "parted company politically."[9]

Jackson was pulling off one of his signature maneuvers. While Union
outliers watched, Jackson led his troops as far as Lewiston and then turned up
into the mountains toward Brown's Gap, apparently surrendering the valley to
Union occupation and heading for Richmond. Hotchkiss thought the route to
Lewiston "the worst road I ever saw in the Valley of Virginia." It took "a whole
regiment of men" to lay miles of horizontal logs to make the route a more us-
able corduroy road. No better was the shortcut from Lewiston to Brown's Gap,
part of a network of wagon tracks intended for hauling charcoal and ore to
Mount Vernon Furnace. On May 2 Jackson set up headquarters at the home
of furnace operator John F. Lewis.[10]

It was easier for John F. Lewis to be hospitable since two days earlier a
Confederate quartermaster had paid him more than $1,700 for 282 barrels of
flour from his mill by the river. After the war, Lewis, needing to show he had received no benefits from the Confederacy, testified that Jackson's men and other
Confederates "took large quantities of flour out of my mill at various times,
and took my hay and fodder without paying for any of it, frequently, during the
war." Other family members made similar complaints, many of them no doubt
true. Lunsford Lewis asserted that his father did not yield voluntarily to Con-

federates appropriating supplies but "frequently told them if they got anything they must take it." Yet a few surviving receipts confirm that, when faced with loss of property to passing Confederate armies, members of the Lewis family could set aside their political distaste and accept compensation.[11]

After lunch at John F. Lewis's the next day, May 3, Stonewall Jackson followed the rest of his army through Brown's Gap. Then he did an about face. The following day Jackson's troops, safely over the far side of the Blue Ridge, boarded cars of the Virginia Central Railroad and were carried not east toward Richmond but west, straight back into the Shenandoah Valley. They forged on into the mountains of western Virginia, and four days later joined a smaller Confederate force. At McDowell the Confederates attacked Brig. Gen. Robert H. Milroy's portion of the much larger Union army of western explorer and adventurer Gen. John C. Fremont and sent Milroy reeling northward. During the next two weeks, the size of Jackson's army nearly doubled—to some 16,000—with arrival of a division of reinforcements under Gen. Richard S. Ewell.[12]

Confederate Gen. T. J. "Stonewall" Jackson made his headquarters at Lewiston on April 30 and May 1, 1862, as he feinted a retreat toward Richmond.

On May 23 Jackson smashed a federal force at Front Royal and went on seventeen miles to take Winchester and move toward the Potomac, frightening residents of Washington. Then Jackson did another about face. Slipping between Union pursuers, he led his army back up along the western side of Massanutten, Fremont in pursuit. But up the far side of Massanutten—the eastern side—came the Union troops of Gen. James Shields. Fremont and Shields expected to trap Jackson at the southern end of the mountain, near Port Republic.[13]

Movements of tens of thousands of battling soldiers were not kind to the countryside. "A more beautiful country than this Valley of the Shenandoah God's sun never smiled on," Charles H. Webb reported in the *New York Times* in June 1862. "The scenery is magnificent, but not with sterile peaks and frowning rocks. Green vestured fields and gentle round-bosomed hills nestle down in the arms of great mountains, and you know they are quick with growing life even while they slumber.

"It rather moves me to sympathy to see the trail of devastation that the two armies have left after them. Meadows of clover are trodden into mud; the tossing plumes of the wheat fields along the line of march are shorn down, as though a thousand reaping machines had passed over and through them. Dead horses lie along the road, entirely overpowering the sweet scent of the clover blossoms. . . . Fences are not, landmarks have vanished and all is one common waste."[14] As the Union army of James Shields approached Lewiston from the same direction Stonewall Jackson's army had scarcely a month before, heavy rains of an unusually wet spring left rivers swollen and turned roadways into seas of mud.

A brigade under Col. Samuel Sprigg Carroll managed to reach Lewiston first, early on the morning of Sunday, June 8. His regiments from Indiana and Pennsylvania were leavened by armed Union Loyalists making up the 1st Virginia (Union) Cavalry. Some cavalrymen made a quick foray into Port Republic. Jackson had his headquarters there at Madison Hall, built by early settler John Madison, brother-in-law of Thomas Lewis and Gabriel Jones and then the home of one of Samuel Hance Lewis's best friends, Union Loyalist Dr. George W. Kemper. Carroll's cavalrymen nearly seized the long bridge separating Jackson's headquarters from his army on the far side, a span critical to the Union plan of joining Fremont's and Shields's armies to trap Jackson's. They came close to seizing Jackson himself.[15]

Having revealed their location, the Union cavalrymen fell back to Lewiston. Colonel Carroll's troops melted into the wooded foothills above until Gen. Erastus B. Tyler arrived with regiments from Ohio. Since Shields was still on his way, it was Tyler who assumed local command from Carroll. Tyler determined that his best defensive position below Port Republic was across the road east of Lewiston, where a knoll at the base of the foothills had lately been cleared as a coaling to make charcoal for Mount Vernon Furnace, four miles up the mountain. John F. Lewis had not run the iron furnace long enough to cut much of the family's adjoining timber to burn into charcoal, so hills above this unusually open and elevated position were still thick with trees and undergrowth. Tyler's chief of artillery, Col. Philip Daum, moved up some guns to the coaling to be ready to sweep the fields below.[16]

As the verdant valley floor sloped gently downward toward the Shenandoah from Lewiston and the newly placed artillery, a dozen homes, outbuildings, and the gristmill spread closer to the river within a mile and a half of each other. At the northern edge of the neighborhood was the onetime home of John F. Lewis—who had moved with his family to Mount Vernon Furnace—and, across a lane, the home of Richard P. Fletcher Jr., 40, who had a medical exemption from the Confederate Army. He was running Lynnwood a half mile away for his niece, Anne Lewis Walton, 21, who had recently inherited her ancestral home.

Some 400 yards west of Lynnwood and nearer the river lived the family of Samuel H. Lewis Jr., near Abraham L. Wagner, 33, a Union Loyalist who ran the mill next door. Three-quarters of a mile southwest, along the edge of the river plain, was the home of Charles H. Lewis. Across a lane were the Winfield Scott Baughers, living in Westwood, the handsome frame house built by Samuel Hance Lewis's uncle Benjamin. Baugher, 32, who leaned toward the Union, had been with the militia in Winchester but was avoiding conscription by paying for a substitute to serve in his place.[17]

As more Federal troops reached Lewiston, some Confederate soldiers could be glimpsed across the river near Cross Keys, their artillery glistening in the sunlight. Once Jackson engaged Fremont at Cross Keys that morning, the sound of cannon fire reached Bogota, overlooking Lewiston and Lynnwood from a ridge on the Cross Keys side of the river. The two-story, ten-room Greek Revival brick home had been built fifteen years earlier by Jacob

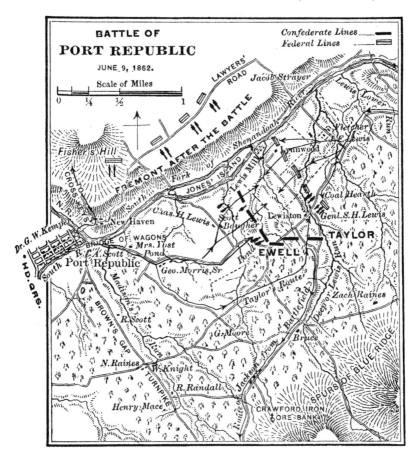

Strayer, now a Confederate partisan. The artillery fire seemed to daughter Clara Strayer a "most terrific cannonading, that waked the mountain echoes that had slept for ages, perhaps had never waked before!" Waves of thunder from dueling batteries reverberated across the river throughout the day, until the Battle of Cross Keys ended at sundown and Fremont withdrew.[18]

As darkness fell, Confederates victorious at Cross Keys could look across the Shenandoah to the flickering campfires of the 3,000 federal soldiers who overflowed the Lewises' fields and woodlands. Some of the flames were consuming Samuel H. Lewis Jr.'s fence rails, for fences were a ready source of seasoned firewood for armies on the move. A thousand rails had been taken along more than a half-mile of his fence lines, an amount equal to ten cords of firewood. One soldier went into his stable and rode off on a four-year-old mare; another took a seven-year-old horse. A complaint to Colonel Carroll brought the promise of payment the next day.[19]

As he sat on the Lewiston portico on the eve of the Battle of Port Republic, Union Col. Samuel Sprigg Carroll promised Samuel Hance Lewis quick payment for corn requisitioned at Lewiston.

Up at Lewiston, patriarch Samuel Hance Lewis got a similar assurance from the colonel as the two sat on the portico that afternoon. In this case, Carroll was taking the 600 bushels of corn that nearly filled Lewiston's crib, leaving "nothing but the shattered corn," a present-day equivalent loss of more than $13,000. Concerned about the risk of the sort of unauthorized seizures occurring at smaller places in the neighborhood—Scott Baugher at Westwood lost five horses and four mares—and aware of the Lewises' loyalties, Carroll posted guards around Lewiston.[20]

At Lynnwood that evening, tension was high among non-Unionist family members, who did not include Anne Lewis Walton's Confederate chaplain husband, away in Georgia. She and her Fletcher relatives were not pleased that the house was "filled with Union officers . . . of every grade." The good news of the day was that Anne Walton's brother-in-law, Abner, and his cousin, John Fletcher, both Confederate infantrymen, were unscathed from the combat at Cross Keys, though that word may not yet have crossed the river.[21]

Nor was the family's mood helped by having Union officers seated at the dinner table. One, Col. Lewis P. Buckley, 58, regimental commander of the 29th Ohio Volunteers, was in particularly fine fettle. They had come to destroy everything that would give comfort to the enemy, he told his hosts, and would do it if it took ten years. But he thought it shouldn't take that long. "By sundown tomorrow night we will have sent Jackson and his army to hell!" Anne Walton's aunt, Susan Fletcher, couldn't help retorting that he shouldn't feel so sure; Buckley himself might be the first to get there. "Oh," said Buckley, "we have Jackson sewed up in a bag, and have only to pull the strings to have him tight!"[22]

With their home occupied, a hostile army camped around them, sounds of the battle across the river still ringing in their ears, and the outlook for the next day not promising, it seemed wise to get Lynnwood's three infants and their mothers to a safer place. Mildred Muse Walton was not yet a year and a half, Margaret Anne Walton was hardly six months, and their mother, Anne Lewis Walton, was expecting a third child in five months. Anne Walton's aunt, Annie Mayhew Fletcher, had given birth to a daughter, Margaret, only the day before. That night Annie Fletcher and her baby were carried from Lynnwood on their bed and escorted to the river by slave women wrapping necessities in their aprons, Anne Walton and her two daughters in tow. The river was so high that it could not be forded, and only flat-bottomed boats could cross. In one, Annie Fletcher's feather mattress was laid for her and day-old Margaret. All were rowed across and made it safely up the ridge to Bogota, where they could spend the night in peace.[23]

Confederate engineers at Port Republic spent most of the night building a wagon bridge across South River, a few hundred yards before it merges with North River to form the Shenandoah's South Fork. The bridge would allow Confederates to move quickly across the swollen river and northward to face the Union army at Lewiston. Before daybreak, Jackson began moving his 6,000 troops from the Cross Keys battlefield southward across North River into Port Republic and across the South Fork, then burned the North River bridge to keep out of reach of Fremont's army.

"The morning was a cool but gorgeous one, with temperatures in the 50s," the coolest day of the month, writes Robert K. Krick. "Many participants commented on the still, pastoral loveliness of the Valley early on June 9." The family at Lewiston was sitting down to breakfast at 7:30 when cannon fire roared from the Union battery atop the coaling across the way. Samuel Hance Lewis, his wife, and younger family members immediately rose, left the house, and headed for the river, where they were joined by the rest of the Fletchers from Lynnwood and by Samuel H. Lewis Jr. and his wife and their four year-old daughter, Lucy. It took the slave oarsmen three crossings to ferry all refugees to the far side.[24]

Once ashore, Unionists and non-Unionists alike were welcomed at Bogota. The columned portico's second-story balcony offered a broad vista across the Shenandoah to the fields of the unfolding battle, the distant peaks of the

Lewis family members were rowed across the Shenandoah to Bogota, home of the Jacob Strayers, supporters of the Confederacy, and watched from its upper verandah as the Battle of Port Republic swept around their homes.

Blue Ridge providing a dramatic backdrop through the morning haze. Clara Strayer was already out on the balcony with her spyglass as the first "stream of fire issued from the cannons' mouth" at the battery above Lewiston, scarcely three-fourths of a mile from where she stood. The targets were "a party of horsemen grouped . . . on the rise below the Lewiston house, where the road goes up to the mountain." They were the vanguard of Stonewall Jackson's nearly 6,000 troops, who were following the river down from Port Republic.[25]

"At first we saw (with the aid of a glass) every movement of the enemy," wrote Clara Strayer, "but as the battle progressed the view was somewhat obscured by smoke." Much of the infantry fire could be seen coming from the Confederate lines in the direction of Westwood—to the right of the view from Bogota's balcony—which the Scott Baughers had the foresight to leave early to stay with relatives near Weyer's Cave. Through a spyglass, the Fletchers took delight as they saw a figure they identified as Col. Lewis Buckley—their obnoxious dinner companion of the night before—shot from his horse. They may never have realized it was a case of mistaken identity; Buckley, not that victim, went on to other battles and died at home in Ohio three years after the war ended. Fighting spread up through the orchards and wheat fields toward Lewiston. Federal troops moved forward from their encampment around Lynnwood to their front line along the fenced lane between Lewiston and the river.[26]

The pivotal point of battle was the Lewiston coaling, a position described as "one of the strongest held by a defensive force during the war." The artillery battery anchored the Union army's left, while the Shenandoah anchored its right. Six artillery pieces were clustered atop the coaling and up an adjacent wooded rise. Their fire repeatedly halted attempts of Confederates in the fields below to advance. Finally, under the guidance of mapmaker Jed Hotchkiss, Confederate soldiers slashed their way undetected through the thickets above before the Union artillerymen below could move their guns around and return the fire. "It was an anxious moment for us," wrote Clara Strayer, "though the suspense was of short duration, [for] we soon saw the glitter of bayonets of reinforcements and heard the shout of victory, which none knew how to give better than our own brave Confederates." By about 10:30 a.m., three hours after it began, the combat ended. The Union army—promises of payment for fence rails, horses, and corn unkept—was in full retreat.[27]

Just arriving on the scene down from Port Republic was the 10th Virginia, so many of its soldiers from Rockingham County—including, in Company B, some from the Port Republic area itself. One of those was William M. Lewis, 27, the only one of Samuel Hance Lewis's five sons to don the Confederate gray. Passing hundreds of dead and wounded strewn across his family's fields while gunsmoke still drifted around the old home as injured soldiers were carried in would have been a sobering experience.[28]

Jackson's soldiers chased the retreating Federals for some eight miles, gathering prisoners until they reached the main force of Union Gen. James Shields and stopped. By sundown, the last of the pursuers returned through a cold rain to Lewiston. Union Gen. John C. Fremont, isolated on the far side of the river by the burned bridge at Port Republic, moved some artillery to the ridge near Bogota. Though his guns could not reach Confederates near Lewiston, the frustrated Fremont shelled the closer part of the battlefield anyway, ignoring the yellow flag flying from Lynnwood to warn that it was a hospital.[29]

Having repulsed two Union armies in two days, Stonewall Jackson took time to consolidate. His supply train rolled from Port Republic up the Brown's Gap Turnpike. Soldiers at the battlefield took the shortcut up from Lewiston, along the same coal roads they had taken five weeks earlier when Jackson made his feint of leaving the valley. Troops camped on the slope of the mountain. Some returned to the battlefield to move the wounded, bury the dead, and collect discarded weapons. Cavalry units reoccupied Harrisonburg and checked out the surrounding region.[30]

At Mount Vernon Furnace, on the day of the battle many Confederate soldiers went to John F. Lewis's home looking for food. In the evening, Jackson's staff rode up and asked to make headquarters there, though Jackson himself would spend that night at the foot of the mountain, on the lookout for the enemy. Five weeks before, the home had been Jackson's headquarters for one night; this time it would be headquarters for three nights. Jackson's ordnance officer William Allan was camped along the road between the furnace and the Lewis house. The family feared his cannons would be placed at the crest of Brown's Gap, and then, if Union troops came up in pursuit, the house would be within their range of fire. "A few months ago," John F. Lewis's sister-in-law wrote in Staunton, "nothing would have appeared more improbable than that sequestered spot would be the battlefield of two large armies."[31]

Those fears did not materialize, and there was no battle at Mount Vernon Furnace. But breakfast conversation in the Lewis home did take a sharp turn one morning. John F. Lewis and his family were at the table with, among others, Stonewall Jackson and his mapmaker, Maj. Jed Hotchkiss, who had grown up near Binghamton, New York and moved to Augusta County as a teacher when he was 19. Hotchkiss remarked to Jackson, in an exultant tone: "Well, General, the Yankees have taken all of George Chrisman's cattle." Chrisman happened to be a lifelong friend of the Lewis family and a Union Loyalist. John F. Lewis's wife, Serena, seated at the head of the table, asked Hotchkiss, "Why do you seem to rejoice so much at Mr. Chrisman's loss?" Hotchkiss replied, "Because he is a traitor to the state." Serena shot back: "If Mr. Chrisman is a traitor to his state then you are a double traitor, because you were born in a northern state and [are] a traitor to your state and the national government."[32]

Hotchkiss, left with little to say, did not record the incident in his journal, and it is not known how much longer the breakfast lasted. Hotchkiss did write that he and Jackson left the Lewis home "at an early hour" on June 12 and spent that night near the river in the valley below. On June 18 Jackson's army once again crossed the Blue Ridge, this time actually headed for new battles in eastern Virginia.[33]

Civilians touched by the sweep of passing armies and the terror of battle could not pack up and leave. In the Battle of Port Republic, 1,000 Union troops were killed, wounded, or missing, as were 800 on the Confederate side. Uncounted numbers of wounded had to be left behind, to be dealt with mostly by dislocated civilians returning to their homes. Lynnwood, once behind federal lines, was where many of the Union wounded had been carried. On the day after the battle, once the rain stopped, refugees who were rowed back from Bogota to Lynnwood were greeted by a dead Union soldier propped against a tree, the family's silver spoons sticking from a pocket. Indoors was a houseful of Union invalids, "lying on the floor amidst pools of blood." All seemed to be begging for water. A nurse left by the Union army was carrying a newly deceased soldier down the stairs when he lost his grip and the body slipped over the banister onto the floor. Cursing, the nurse picked up the body, carried it outdoors, and tried to bury it in a shallow hole. Richard Fletcher thought the nurse "altogether useless," sent him out to the field, and buried the soldier himself. Then there was the soldier crazed by a head wound, which Fletcher washed and dressed.[34]

The house itself seems to have been damaged by only one cannonball, which broke through a wall in a bedroom, above Anne Walton's bed. But beds and bedding had been ripped apart, perhaps in a search for hidden valuables. The house was robbed "of everything which they could destroy or take away," including women's dresses and other clothing. Outdoors, cattle and horses were gone, throats were cut on sheep that could not be driven away, and farm utensils were missing. Richard Fletcher took charge while the women stayed at Bogota, crossing the river by day to cook and tend the wounded as they were able.[35]

Lewiston had been hit by a shell that broke through the west wall of the dining room, exploded in a china press and destroyed the family's stock of porcelain ware. As the home behind Confederate lines closest to the heaviest fighting, Lewiston was soon filled with Confederate casualties. Injured Union soldiers went to the barns and sheds. The next day, many area residents went to Lewiston to care for the wounded Confederates, leaving Samuel Hance Lewis, his family, and their slaves to care for the Union wounded in the out-buildings. Neighbors wandering over to the coaling found "over twenty horses . . . dead almost in touch of each other." Lunsford Lewis recognized a dead Union artillery horse as one of those taken from his brother the night before.[36]

Scenes at other homes in the neighborhood—as on battlefields throughout the war—differed little. The Scott Baughers returned to Westwood to find a ditch beside the road turned into a mass grave, with bodies thrown in and covered with dirt. Cannonballs had struck chimneys, and the home was filled with the wounded. Sheets, towels, and linens had been torn into bandages.[37]

The *Rockingham Register* lavished columns of type on "the numerous outrages perpetrated upon our people by Lincoln's army," though the paper concluded that "time and space would fail us to recount all the thefts and robberies committed. . . . [Union soldiers] seemed all to be upon a regularly organized plundering expedition in the name of the government and under the protection of the flag of the late United States." Left unchronicled were comments of those who would later claim that the Confederate Army took as much "or more" than the Union Army.[38]

What was regarded as human property in the South was perplexing for the Union army. It found itself facing, at one point, "a stampede" of slaves seeking refuge behind their lines, but guidelines on how to deal with them seemed imprecise. The *Rockingham Register* was happy to report on two young slaves, one belonging to Jacob Strayer and the other to Samuel Hance Lewis. The pair went off with the retreating Union Army as wagoneers, "but say they never received a cent for their services." They were told, instead, to "steal their wages from the rebels. Becoming tired of such freedom and such respectability as the Yankee government secured them, they gave their new friends 'leg bail' a few days ago, and by the kindness of Southern gentlemen are now both at their old homes."[39]

As the Lewis family dealt with the battle's aftermath, Annie Fletcher's baby, born the day before the battle, survived the rigors of the time, but Anne Lewis Walton's infant daughter, Margaret Anne, did not. Unable to face the devastation at Lynnwood, Anne Walton left her refuge at Bogota to stay with relatives at Broadway until the birth of her third daughter in November. She then took her two surviving daughters to join her chaplain husband in Georgia, leaving Lynnwood in charge of her uncle, Richard Fletcher Jr.[40]

At Lewiston, Samuel Hance Lewis maintained the equilibrium that had seen his family through the war thus far. In December he had a visit from a second cousin twice removed, Robert T. Barton, 20, of Winchester, a private with the Second Virginia during the battle who found himself traveling in the neighborhood six months later while on duty. "I had often heard my parents speak of Gen. Lewis and I determined to pay him a visit," Barton wrote. He was aware that "the General and all his family were strong Union people, altho one of his sons was in the Confederate Army. This, however, did not interfere with the kindly treatment which I received, and I enjoyed the visit very much." The two crossed the river to Bogota to visit the graves of Barton's great-great grandparents, Gabriel Jones and Margaret Strother Jones, Samuel Hance Lewis's great-aunt who had contributed to his Bible Society fund drive so many years before.[41]

Barton wrote of having seen Lewiston during the battle and of events of his visit six months later. In the afternoon, he wrote of his time with his older cousin, "We walked together over the battle field, where the hogs had rooted up the dead, and bones and skulls lay thick around." They found "my friendly apple tree" and counted the seven holes from bullets that struck the tree while Barton took refuge behind it during the height of the battle. He was shown where the shell passed through Lewiston's west wall and exploded in the china press. "From the direction from which the shot came, it was very probable that it was fired by my own battery," Barton realized. He confessed to Samuel Hance Lewis, "but that only furnished a theme for jokes at the table that night, and he seemed to feel no anger about it."[42]

4

John F. Lewis's Private War

Friction between Confederates and Union Loyalists flared as war engulfed the South. In Richmond, the outspoken former congressman John Minor Botts, among more than fifty Union Loyalists jailed early in 1862, was banished from the city. Guerilla bands of Unionists fought Confederates in the Piedmont Quaker Belt of North Carolina, the Piney Woods of Mississippi, and the Big Thicket of East Texas. Secret Unionist societies were formed in Alabama, Florida, and North Texas, where, in Cooke County, sixty-five members of one group were hung, a third of them without trial. In Atlanta, as many as one hundred Union Loyalists "began to learn how to live under conditions of silence, isolation and pressure unlike anything they had ever known."[1]

Union Loyalists in Virginia's Rockingham County kept in touch informally, if not as an organized group. "Those of us who were Union men frequently had conferences during the continuance of the war," remembered Harrisonburg lawyer William J. Points, "and discussed among ourselves the sentiments of the leading men in the various counties around here." Samuel Hance Lewis's brother Charles said of his Port Republic neighbor William D. Maiden: "We knew each other as decidedly Union men, and had no fear to express ourselves freely to each other." For those not as well acquainted, Rockingham Loyalists shared some secret sign so they "knew each other without much talk."[2]

Conflict was complicated in northern and western Rockingham by Virginia's greatest concentration of pacifist Mennonites and Brethren, most of German origin and part of the largest such regional community in the South. The Confederate government ultimately exempted them from military duty if they would pay higher taxes, but in the meantime they were pressured into service. One, Benjamin Bowman, was roped to his horse in Dayton and led to Harrisonburg. There, his hands tied, he was forced into a wagon with his brother Isaac and carried off to join the southern army, even though many Mennonites and Brethren made to carry rifles refused to fire them at "the enemy." At least two groups trying to flee North with the aid of local guides were captured and imprisoned. Although shunning or exile would be the worst fate of most outspoken Unionists in the Shenandoah Valley, one Brethren activist in Rockingham County, Elder John Kline, was murdered beside the road near his Broadway home.[3]

After Kline's death came the oft-muttered threat, "Colonel Gray next!" Rockingham Secession Convention delegate Algernon Gray may have finally cast his vote in favor of secession at Richmond, but he was still resented for his ongoing loyalty to the Union. Gray yielded to the pleas of his daughters and fled to Baltimore for the duration of the war.[4]

In their rural setting, the Samuel Hance Lewises were away from populous Harrisonburg's concentration of antagonists, and remained as discreet and inoffensive as they could be to avoid trouble. "I was never arrested," John F. Lewis could say after the war ended. "I think it providential I was not. One of Jackson's staff told me that Jackson was advised to have me arrested as a prisoner of state but refused, on the ground that I had committed no overt act of disloyalty to the Confederacy."[5]

No amount of discretion, however, could prevent unpleasantness. Of his brother Samuel Jr., Lunsford Lewis recalled: "In common with my father and the family, he was frequently denounced and threatened with imprisonment for his Union sentiments." Though Lunsford was himself "frequently abused for expressing Union sentiments," with the energy of his mid-teens he "always returned it in kind and considered it even." Two miles away in Port Republic, William Maiden was "threatened dozens of times, was told I ought to be driven from the country, that no damned Union son of a bitch should live in this country, that they ought to be shot down like dogs and they would not be allowed to stay here when the war was over, and such like expressions. I could name a dozen persons who have threatened me to my face." He was held "in duress" by one critic for more than a day for being "a dangerous Union man."[6]

William Maiden's plight was like that of many unwilling or unable to flee their homes for the safety of Union territory. "At the beginning of the war I had a wife and two little daughters," he said. "I had no means at all to convey them beyond the lines of the Confederacy and no means of supporting them, or I would have done it."[7]

He did know John F. Lewis. As an owner of Mount Vernon Furnace, sequestered halfway up the western slope of the Blue Ridge, Lewis had the power of granting military exemptions to those working in the critical iron industry. Maiden went looking for a job at the furnace, but John F. Lewis had another idea. Maiden was a cooper, and Lewis, not overly concerned with following Confederate government rules, needed a cooper to make barrels at the family flour mill by the river. On paper, Maiden was assigned to the furnace to make him exempt from the Confederate Army. Then Lewis "put a trusted slave of his to take my place at the furnace and put me to work as a cooper for his mill."[8]

Local Confederates scorned John F. Lewis as an opportunist not above perverting the laws of the new government of the land. He was thought "disingenuous" for expressing Unionist beliefs as it suited him while providing iron for the Confederacy, avoiding military service himself in the process. The irony, many believed, was that by supplying "munitions of war," his iron furnace workers "rendered possibly more aid to the Confederate service than the same number armed with muskets."[9]

Local Union Loyalists, on the other hand, saw employment by John F. Lewis as a refuge from reprehensible Confederate military duty and as a legal way to stay close to their families in perilous times. He was respected for being as adept at pulling a local Confederate soldier out of a distant guardhouse and putting him to work at the furnace as he was at keeping a wrongly accused Loyalist from being shot by the Union Army. Plus, the majority of his iron apparently went for civilian rather than direct military purposes.

As the war dragged on, other Virginia iron furnaces were complaining of manpower shortages. But so many Union Loyalists were pleading for employment at Mount Vernon Furnace that the sympathetic John F. Lewis overstaffed his operation. That left so little for some workers to do that he simply let them stay home, thereby still denying them to the Confederate Army. Mount Vernon Furnace, thought Brethren preacher John Harshbarger, was "merely a shelter for Union men to keep them from the Army."[10]

John F. Lewis was conducting, in effect, his own private war.

A deep network of family ties helped provide John F. Lewis with the opportunity to avoid Confederate military service by taking over Mount Vernon Furnace, and thus be able not only to stay home with his family but also to prosper, thanks to the sudden rebirth of Virginia's iron industry. His connection with the region's iron industry went back three generations. On his mother's side, he was a great-grandson of Henry "Iron Man" Miller, an ironmaster who came from Pennsylvania to Virginia in 1774 and built a pioneering iron furnace and two forges on ore-rich land beside Mossy Creek in northeastern Augusta County.

After Miller's death, his son Samuel—John F. Lewis's great-uncle—expanded the operation into nearby Rockingham County. Ore had been found not far from South River, some three miles upstream from where it joined the Shenandoah's South Fork at Port Republic. In 1810, beside South River near the community later named Grottoes, Samuel Miller put up what became known as Mount Vernon Forge, plus a small furnace nearby to process iron for the forge. Miller's Forge Road was built to connect Mossy Creek Iron Works with Mount Vernon Forge. After Samuel Miller died in 1830, Mount Vernon Forge was taken over by John Miller, 32.[11]

Mount Vernon Forge had the advantage of ready access to distant markets. Once the New Shenandoah Company cleared the river for shipping downstream from Port Republic to the Potomac in the 1820s, obstructions were cleared from Port Republic as far upstream as the forge. Then, in the late 1840s, work was authorized to enlarge the road from Harrisonburg over the Blue Ridge to Charlottesville into a highway called Brown's Gap Turnpike. Three miles into the mountains the route crossed a nineteen-mile belt of high-grade brown hematite ore. With the better road more easily traveled by heavy wagons, it did not take John Miller long to see the opportunity of building a furnace near the ore banks and hauling smelted iron down the turnpike to Mount Vernon Forge for processing, then shipping it down the river.[12]

To build and manage the furnace, in 1847 John Miller lured ironmaster William G. Miller, 41—son of Mount Vernon Forge founder Samuel Miller and a first cousin of John F. Lewis's mother—back from Missouri, where many members of the Miller family had emigrated. Apparently following the tradition of naming a furnace for a female family member, William Miller named it Margaret Jane Furnace, most likely for his eldest daughter, Margaret, 15. Margaret Jane Furnace was in full operation by 1849 and "in blast" six months of the year, its fires extinguished for maintenance and winter weather. Five years later the furnace had reached an annual production of 750 tons. After being hauled down to Mount Vernon Forge, much of the raw iron was re-formed into 300-pound blooms—spongy masses of wrought iron—and boated down the Shenandoah. The rest was further refined and forged on site—with the aid of eight fires and two water-powered hammers—into wrought iron implements for local use.[13]

This was a profitable time for charcoal-fueled iron furnaces in Virginia. In the South, the state had become a close second to Alabama in iron production, thanks to ore discoveries elsewhere around the Shenandoah Valley and on the western slopes of the Blue Ridge. At least fifty furnaces were built in Virginia between the mid-1820s and the early 1850s, doubling the state's iron output. They easily competed with charcoal furnaces in Pennsylvania, and high tariffs protected them from competition with imported iron. But in the mid-1850s Pennsylvania furnaces started switching their fuel from charcoal to locally available anthracite and became highly competitive. Many Virginia furnaces began shutting down.[14]

Unlike many of the closed furnaces, John Miller's had the advantage of close access to high-grade ore. He rebuilt his forge in 1855 and kept the furnace busy. But competition seems to have reduced his profit margin; he fell behind in paying his debts and became insolvent. In September 1857 the sheriff held liens against Miller totaling more than $10,000, today's equivalent of $250,000. If executed, they could cause his furnace, despite its steady business, to close. Augusta County friends and relatives came to the rescue.[15]

Staunton attorney John B. Baldwin structured the deal. Merchant and banker Benjamin Crawford, 56—a cousin of John Miller's wife, Mary—and Joseph Smith paid the lien holders, avoiding foreclosure and a shutdown.[16] They converted indebtedness from their payments into shares of a trust set up by Baldwin. Miller signed title to all his business and personal assets to the trust, thus holding remaining creditors at bay. As trustee, Baldwin would oversee operation of the forge and furnace. John Miller and his furnace manager, William G. Miller, were to remain in place until ownership changed. An independent appraisal assigned to Samuel Hance Lewis and two of his close friends, Dr. George W. Kemper and Stephen Harnsberger, estimated the worth of the iron operation at $48,900—adjusted for inflation, nearly $1.3 million in present-day currency.[17]

In January 1859, Baldwin oversaw the sale of John Miller's personal property to defray Miller's indebtedness. But no buyer came forward to offer anything close to the appraised value of the furnace. In December, Crawford and Smith, realizing that they might never recoup the amount of their original investment, converted their shares in the trust to direct ownership of the operation.[18] Although published chronologies of Margaret Jane Furnace do not report it closing during this period, no ironmaster is recorded in Rockingham County in the census of 1860, suggesting that the dozen forge and furnace hands listed as residing nearby were presiding over a reduced operation, if not one soon shut down altogether.[19]

Within a few years competition with less expensive iron from Pennsylvania had reduced the number of Virginia's functioning charcoal-fueled iron furnaces by three-fourths, leaving only fourteen by 1860. The state's annual output had fallen to 9,096 tons. But the South's major ordnance plant—Richmond's Tredegar Iron Works—would need 15,000 tons of iron a year to supply munitions makers throughout the Confederacy. Iron from Pennsylvania and overseas could not reach Richmond through Union lines and blockades, and transportation difficulties made importing iron from other southern states virtually impossible. In fall 1861, Tredegar Iron Works President Joseph Reid Anderson appealed to owners of twenty-one Virginia furnaces that could be reopened with minimal work. He based his plea not just on Southern patriotism but on the premise that iron furnaces now provided "the business chance of a lifetime."[20]

Mount Vernon Furnace had a stone stack like that pictured at the rear of Liberty Furnace in neighboring Shenandoah County, and a similar production capacity as well.

John F. Lewis had no shortage of access to inside assessments of Margaret Jane Furnace. His cousin had run it, his father had appraised it, and a fellow Unionist delegate to the Secession Convention—John B. Baldwin of Staunton—had restructured its finances. Threats of those wishing to hang him for his negative vote on secession were still ringing in his ears, and, indeed, were still being made. John F. Lewis moved his family four miles to a home up in the densely wooded mountains, went into the iron business, and signed a contract with Joseph R. Anderson & Co., parent company of Tredegar Iron Works, "that paid handsomely."[21]

Margaret Jane Furnace was renamed Mount Vernon Furnace to match the name of the forge by the river. Its operating entity was designated Lewis, Crawford & Company after the new lead principals. Crawford was James Crawford, 28, oldest son of previous major owner Benjamin Crawford and son-in-law of the furnace's original ironmaster, William G. Miller. The two went looking for an experienced supervisor. They found him in Manasseh Blackburn, 43, an ironmaster who had moved from Pennsylvania to neighboring ore-rich Shenandoah County in 1858. Blackburn was recruited with the promise of an ownership interest and moved to Rockingham County in early 1862.[22]

The focal point of the operation—at 1,300 feet, halfway up to Brown's Gap—was a structure of classic charcoal iron furnace design. Mount Vernon

Furnace's truncated stone pyramid featured a chimney tapering upward to 31 feet from the rear top of the base of a vertical stack approximately 25 feet square. At the front top of the base, ingredients were dumped in; with every 100 pounds of iron ore were mixed some 6 bushels of charcoal and 40 pounds of limestone. As the mix fell through the stack, the fire was brought to more than 2,000 degrees by blasts of air from bellows, their lifting and falling regulated by cogs on a waterwheel powered by flow diverted from Madison's Run.

On the surface of the melting mass, the limestone's chemical makeup drew impurities from the iron to form slag, quickly skimmed off and discarded. The inverse pyramid of the stack's interior focused the molten iron onto a hearth floor only a few feet in diameter, keeping the mass sufficiently dense so it would not solidify until after it had flowed outside through the casting arch into a main trench and off, at right angles, into a series of smaller side trenches. The finished arrangement was so similar to that of a litter of suckling piglets that the hardened ingots were dubbed "pig iron." To keep the furnace in blast, the sequence had to be maintained around the clock, in twelve-hour shifts.[23]

Surrounding the belching, fiery leviathan and its heaps of slag was a community of shops, sheds, stables, and cottages for the hundred or more free and slave laborers. To fuel the furnace, some workers cut timber on the property's 23,000 acres at the rate of more than an acre a day. Logs were hauled to scattered open areas known as coalings, where they were stacked by colliers for slow and careful burning, in weeklong cycles, into charcoal. Wagonloads of charcoal—far lighter than wagonloads of logs—were hauled along networks of rutted roadways to the furnace.

Other workers mined the ore and limestone. Ore broken up at one bank—100 feet farther up the slope—was loaded into cars drawn down rail tracks to the furnace by gravity; empty cars were pulled back up the tracks by horses or mules. Wagons carried in more ore from another major bank five miles north and from others down the mountains. Wagoneers hauled the finished pig iron down the turnpike.[24]

Of the twenty-one iron furnaces urged at the start of the war to reopen, twenty did so. Virginia's iron production soared to 20,000 tons a year, quite enough to cover projected military needs. John F. Lewis stated that the Confederacy "forcibly claimed and took a portion" of all the iron Mount Vernon Furnace produced. Surviving records for mid-1863 indicate that a weekly average of approximately six tons of bar iron went to the Confederate Army's ordnance depot at Staunton—about 20 percent of Mount Vernon's prewar average weekly production. Since with a full complement of labor during the

In a scene similar to those at Mount Vernon Furnace, miners at Elizabeth Furnace in Shenandoah County dig from an ore bank in the 1870s.

war Mount Vernon would have been running close to capacity, that calculation suggests much more iron was being produced for civilian purposes than for military use.[25]

Elsewhere, however, labor shortages and transportation problems were slowing Virginia's spurt of iron making. To increase the reliability of its iron supply, the Confederate Army was running a furnace it had built in Botetourt County, sixty miles from Mount Vernon. Confederate officials threatened to put the army in charge of Mount Vernon Furnace, too, if Lewis and Crawford did not cancel the contract with Joseph R. Anderson & Co.—parent company of Tredegar Iron Works—and sign one on better terms directly with the Confederate government, which had taken over the Richmond Armory and begun forging some of its own ordnance there.[26]

John F. Lewis and ironmaster Manasseh Blackburn talked things over. "We thought it better for us to hold the works than to let the rebel government send people there themselves to work them," recalled Blackburn. By being able "to keep hands out of the army," he said, "we thought that we were doing less for the Confederacy that way than if we let the government use the works themselves." They agreed in fall 1863. John F. Lewis was careful to stress that he did not sign voluntarily, but was persuaded to do so by friends "to shield me from the threatened violence of the secessionists." He later vehemently denied "that I ever made a pound of iron for the purpose of aiding the Confederate cause."[27]

The Confederate government's coercion of John F. Lewis to sign the new contract may have been motivated less by a need to control iron production at an already dependable furnace than by annoyance at knowing of the Union Loyalist shelter provided by Mount Vernon. That hint comes from an issue raised in the congressional election campaign of 1865 between John F. Lewis and Alexander H. H. Stuart. Stuart's allies were "circulating a report" that the Confederate government had considered canceling the original contract on the grounds of disloyalty and that Lewis had to go to Richmond to prove his loyalty, though Lewis declared the report "entirely false."[28]

In any event, by not letting the Confederacy take direct control of Mount Vernon Furnace, decisions on whom to hire remained with John F. Lewis— "the strongest kind of a Union man," thought Loyalist iron worker Levi Pirkey of Mill Creek, one who did "all he could to prevent persons from going into the army and helped those trying to keep out." Port Republic Union Loyalist Amos Scott's son Michael, 20, was conscripted, but, said a grateful Amos Scott, "Lewis got him out for me, and he hauled for the iron works," though they had "the understanding that he should help me on the farm part of the time so I could make something to support my family." As it turned out, Michael said, "I stayed home all the time, except doing a little hauling occasionally with the ore team for the furnace."[29]

Confederate authorities chased down Union Loyalist Lawrence Crawford of Port Republic, conscripted him, and sent him to join troops at Fredericksburg, where he wound up in the guardhouse. John F. Lewis got him out to work at the furnace. Lawrence Crawford's brother Henry "was dragged from the cellar of our house by conscript officers and sent to Mount Jackson early in the war," remembered their sister Martha. "He soon ran away, came home and dodged about in the woods, and finally got John F. Lewis to get him detailed to work at the furnace, so they never got him again." Some sought to retaliate against the Crawfords by going after their horses but found none. The horses were in use up at the furnace.[30]

George Miller of Goods Mill, like William Maiden, was officially assigned to the furnace but worked at the Lewis gristmill down at the river. Since its workload was not steady, Miller was pleased to be able to spend "a great part of the time at home." Andrew J. Baugher of Mill Creek was assigned to the furnace but stayed home altogether.[31]

The grateful workers were well aware, as Lawrence Crawford observed, that Lewis and Blackburn "had a good many more men detailed than they needed." As marauding Union armies headed up the valley in 1864, burning any enterprise aiding the Confederacy, Manasseh Blackburn suggested to John F. Lewis that they play it safe and close the furnace. But "Lewis objected, saying it would put eighty men in the Confederate Army."[32]

5

North with Sheridan

Stonewall Jackson's victorious campaign in 1862 bought the Shenandoah Valley a respite. Military activity seemed reduced to games of hide-and-seek between Union Loyalists and Confederate conscriptors desperate to corral draft-age men to replace casualties at the front. But civil authority was breaking down. Marauders, said John F. Lewis, "reduced horse-thieving to a science," and "it was almost impossible to recover a stolen horse." He had to hire a guard at his stable.[1]

Over at Bogota, patriarch Jacob Strayer died in March 1863. His family, traumatized by pillaging at their isolated home by Union soldiers the year before, moved from the banks of the Shenandoah to Harrisonburg, where they were close to relatives. But by December they were dealing with unruly soldiers once again. As more Federals came to town, the Strayers were "repeatedly robbed" and had to cook at night, "as the smoke from the chimney was an invitation to the enemy to raid kitchens and larders." Had they known the situation would get so bad, wrote Clara Strayer, "I am sure we would have availed ourselves of the first Northern train."[2]

Arrival of the Union troops in Harrisonburg kept lawyer Charles H. Lewis from court in December 1863. When he could get there a month later from his home near Lewiston there was little business left to attend to. Even more discouraging, "I never go from home now when I can help it. Everything in the country is gloom and despondency." He was rather bitter about it. "The wicked and reckless policy of the dirty demagogues who are legislating away what little lifeblood is left in the body politic is regarded even by those who were the most thoroughgoing secessionists as the recklessness of men in despair." He was ready for a change.[3]

As Union armies tightened their grip on the South in 1864, the fertile Shenandoah Valley—known, if with some overstatement, as the "Breadbasket of the Confederacy"—became once again a prime target. Stonewall Jackson may have put on a brilliant display of speed and daring in driving out invaders two years earlier, but he was dead, and beleaguered Confederate troops were spread thin. The 13,000 Confederates under Gen. Jubal Early, sometimes considered Robert E. Lee's "best corps commander in the Army of Northern

Union Gen. Philip Sheridan's troops follow Confederate Gen. Jubal Early's army up the Shenandoah Valley in this contemporary drawing by Alfred R. Waud, a staff artist for *Harper's Weekly*.

Virginia," showed promise in pushing back Union armies threatening the valley in early summer. But they would find themselves overwhelmed by Maj. Gen. Philip H. Sheridan, U. S. Grant's charismatic cavalry commander of the Army of the Potomac. In August 1864, as crops intended to feed the Confederate Army were ripening, Grant picked Sheridan to lead a 43,000-man Army of the Shenandoah. His assignment was to turn the valley into such "a barren waste" that "crows flying over it for the balance of the season will have to carry their provender with them." Indeed, devastation and dislocation from Sheridan's impending expedition of 1864 proved far worse for the valley than during Stonewall Jackson's campaign of 1862.[4]

Civilians feared their neighborhoods could be engulfed in battles like those of two years before. In June 1864 the army of Union Maj. Gen. David Hunter, who preceded Sheridan, camped two miles from Lewiston. Brothers Lunsford and Samuel H. Lewis Jr. went to Hunter's headquarters in an apparent mission to ensure Hunter knew that he and the Lewises were on the same side. They need not have worried. Remembered Lunsford Lewis: "One of General Hunter's staff stated that he had known my father a good many years and [also] two of his sons. . . . He said he was delighted to hear of his steadfast Unionism, as he did hear all through the Valley." The officers "seemed glad to see us, and asked for information. We gave them such information as we possessed."[5]

NO CAUSE OF OFFENCE

General Sheridan began cautiously, pushing slowly up the valley from Harpers Ferry, at the mouth of the Shenandoah. After five weeks of intermittent combat, on September 22 he routed Confederates not far from Winchester. That opened his way south up the Valley Pike along the western side of Massanutten Mountain to begin "the Burning," a swath of destruction some fifty miles long and twenty-five miles wide from Woodstock on south past Harrisonburg. In lush Rockingham County, Sheridan's men burned 100,000 bushels of wheat and 50,000 bushels of corn; destroyed 6,233 tons of hay; drove off 11,050 cattle, horses, sheep and hogs; and burned 450 barns.[6]

Nor were Union Loyalists necessarily exempt from harsh treatment. Isaac Bowman, who farmed 210 acres near Harrisonburg, could only stand by and watch as his farm was stripped, though he was lucky his barn was not burned. "My five milch cows, six sheep, eight hogs and three young cattle were all in the field together and were driven away by General Sheridan's soldiers," he recounted. "I made no complaint to any officer. . . . My gray horse was at my father-in-law's. I did not see it taken. . . . My 100 bushels of oats were in the granary and were taken out by 1,000 cavalry encamped near my house. The soldiers just carried it out in sacks and fed it to their horses. . . . My twelve acres of corn in the shock were taken. . . . My 3,000 [fence]rails were taken and burned. . . . They were right good rails. . . . My ten tons of hay was taken out of the barn . . . and fed to the horses. An officer came along with the soldiers to get the hay. They said they had to have the hay. . . . My rifle, dried apples and apple butter . . . were in the house and were taken out by the soldiers. There were some officers present. Nothing was said by the officers or soldiers."[7]

Homes were usually safe. But in one egregious incident, Sheridan heard that Lt. John R. Meigs, eldest son of the quartermaster general of the Union Army, was killed near Dayton—sixteen miles northwest of Lewiston—by local citizens, rather than, as turned out to be the case, by Confederate soldiers in the course of war. At once Sheridan ordered all homes within a three-mile radius of the site of Meigs's death to be burned; as their owners stood by helplessly, many were emptied of their contents and set ablaze until the order was rescinded and the town itself was spared. Barns and mills were to be burned only when full. Word came to Samuel Hance Lewis by "grapevine telegraph" that his family's mill would not be burned if its store of grain was taken out by morning. That news was quickly sent on to John F. Lewis at Mount Vernon Furnace. Teams and wagons had become scarce, but the furnace had a good supply. Wagons were sent down, the grain was hauled off during the night to a safe haven near Weyer's Cave, and the mill was spared.[8]

On September 25, Union Brig. Gen. Wesley Merritt's First Cavalry Division moved south from Harrisonburg to Port Republic. Some troops went on to blow up a bridge at Waynesboro. Others drove the main Confederate force up the turnpike toward Brown's Gap. Confederate Gen. Jubal Early set up headquarters at Mount Vernon Furnace. The next morning Confederate Gen. Joseph B. Kershaw's division, coming from the northeast, took Federal artillery fire as it turned south at Lewiston for the side route up to Brown's Gap to join Early. Mapmaker Jed Hotchkiss guided Kershaw's men up the twisting coal roads. Foraging Confederate quartermasters paid Samuel Hance Lewis for twenty-seven bushels of corn and 250 pounds of fodder.[9]

September 29 was a busy day for Merritt's Federals. Some took a twenty-mile swing from Port Republic to Mount Crawford, with a side foray up Brown's Gap Turnpike toward Early, who had withdrawn from Mount Vernon Furnace to the top of the gap. Merritt's men that day drove off 321 head of cattle and 20 sheep; burned 82 barns, 72 stacks of hay and grain, 5 flour mills, and 2 sawmills; and set fire to Mount Vernon Furnace. Lighting that torch fell to the Ninth New York Volunteer Cavalry, from Chautauqua County. The unit's regimental history seems almost apologetic about it: "The 9th N.Y. unfortunately burned the iron works in Brown's Gap belonging to a Mr. Lewis, who was a non-combatant and had refused to join the secessionists." Capt. Edwin Goodrich's company took twenty-five prisoners. A "large force" of Confederate infantrymen, seeing the smoke, came down, but the 9th had left and there was nothing for them to do.[10]

Without Mount Vernon Furnace to employ them, military exemptions of its Union Loyalist workers also went up in the smoke. The men quickly scattered. George Miller got to safety in the newly formed state of West Virginia. William Coleman—"I was liable to conscript and had to keep out of the way"—made it down the mountainside to hide at the Scott Baughers at Westwood for three weeks. He spent much of the time with Baugher in the woods, where their wives brought them food. But they happened to be in the house when conscript officers came by. Coleman hid in the cellar. Baugher was upstairs and was taken off to Richmond.[11]

N. J. Wagner and William Maiden trekked fifteen miles north from the furnace to a mountain refuge at Swift Run Gap "where men, women and children were all Union." Maiden thought the place sufficiently safe to move his family there to live with his brother-in-law, though Maiden and other male fugitives took the precaution for the rest of the war of spending the nights away from home. He described their hideout: "I and another Union man dug a large room in the steep mountainside of a hollow in the Blue Ridge and roofed it with boards, with the slope of the hill, and built a fireplace in the upper end. I have had as many as twenty Union men in that room at night, comfortable and warm, where nobody could discover [us] until they got right on it."[12]

Brothers Henry and Lawrence Crawford took another way out: they left down the valley with Sheridan's departing army.[13]

Flight down the valley also seemed the best option to three members of the Lewiston family at risk of conscription. One was Lunsford Lomax Lewis, 18, who had been managing Lewiston's farming operations, and whose late mother's first cousin, Lunsford Lindsay Lomax, was a Confederate major general commanding a cavalry division not far away. Lunsford Lewis met an advance guard of Sheridan's cavalry along the road and was asked if he was subject to Confederate military duty. Lunsford replied that he was, "and on that account I wanted to go North." Told by the officer in charge that he would have to go to headquarters to see about that, he went, met General Sheridan and "told him who I was and what I wanted to do. He granted me the privilege of going to Harpers Ferry with a detachment of his army, and gave orders that myself and others with me should be properly cared for. He told me he knew my family by reputation and was satisfied with their loyalty to the government."[14]

Brother William M. Lewis, 29, the family's lone Confederate soldier, had already thought better of his decision to enlist. When his 10th Virginia Infantry reached the devastation around his home after the Battle of Port Republic, he went on east with Stonewall Jackson's army. Two months later he was wounded at the Battle of Second Manassas. In November 1862 Private Lewis was detailed to the Nitre Bureau, the Confederacy's response to the blockade of its foreign sources of saltpeter, vital for making gunpowder. The Nitre Bureau supervised saltpeter mines throughout the South, more than two dozen in Virginia alone. Whether it was reluctance to be a miner or disillusionment with the Confederate cause, he soon left for home, where he had, thus far, "succeeded in keeping out of the army."[15]

John F. Lewis's eldest son, Daniel Sheffey Lewis, 20, was assigned to Mount Vernon Furnace. He seems to have planned his exit before losing his exemption, for Lunsford Lewis places the date of their departure to join Sheridan at September 28, the day before the furnace was burned. Joining younger brothers William and Lunsford and nephew Sheffey was Charles H. Lewis, 48, unencumbered by an immediate family and with little left of his law practice. All were made nominal prisoners of the Union Army, gaining them the protection of guards on their journey.[16]

After a week of organizing near Harrisonburg, Sheridan's army began moving back down the valley on the rainy morning of October 6, leaving a campsite of several hundred acres so covered with litter that it looked like "the site of a vanished carnival." Sheridan sent an escort into Harrisonburg to meet Union Loyalist Robert Gray and his family and shepherd them to the safety of the departure area. There they joined the four Lewises and hundreds of other civilians in a refugee train, supplied by 400 wagons, with herds of cattle and sheep swelled by more found along the way. "The wonder is not that so many left," thought the disillusioned Clara Strayer in Harrisonburg, "but that any remained."[17]

As the refugees joined the thousands of soldiers and their wagons, the procession stretched some sixteen miles down the Valley Pike. Guards stayed

on the lookout for shots from bushwhackers and raids by vagrants looking for booty. At about 10 p.m. the procession stopped between New Market and Mount Jackson, having covered twenty-five miles, a quarter of the way to Harpers Ferry. Civilians gathered to sing, and soldiers crowded around to listen. Refugees were up the next morning before dawn, joining wagons and livestock to begin moving northward once again.[18]

Once at Harpers Ferry and safely in Union territory, companions went their separate ways. Former Mount Vernon Furnace worker Lawrence Crawford, who had kept with the Lewises, went to Washington and found a government job. Isaac Bowman, the hapless Union Loyalist whose farm near Harrisonburg had been

Lunsford Lewis left the Shenandoah Valley as a refugee with Sheridan to avoid the risk of conscription into the Confederate Army.

stripped by Sheridan's army, left to spend the rest of the war in Ohio. Another fellow traveler, William S. Downs, had more difficulty. The only man in Port Republic when some Union soldiers were fired on, he was accused of doing the shooting. Only Sheffey Lewis's ardent and timely testimony to Downs's loyalty to the Union kept him from being shot at once. Instead he was escorted under arrest with the refugees to Harpers Ferry and sent on to prison at Point Lookout, where he was finally able to get his case heard and be released three months later.[19]

Charles H. Lewis went to Washington. There he dined with Abraham Lincoln's attorney general, Edward Bates of Missouri, a native Virginian who was keeping in touch with Virginia refugees. Lewis brought Bates up to date on events in the Shenandoah Valley and perhaps also lobbied for one of the government jobs brother William—and, apparently, nephew Sheffey—had until the war ended.[20]

Civilian refugees with Union Gen. Philip Sheridan's wagon train move northward through the early morning mist and smoke toward Harpers Ferry in this October 1864 drawing by Alfred Waud.

Lunsford Lewis took the train to Iowa and stayed with an uncle, Presley Thornton Lomax, who eight years earlier had moved with his wife from eastern Virginia to the prospering Mississippi River port of Keokuk, where he practiced law. In considering how Lunsford could best spend his time in exile, college seemed a good option. Presley Lomax was a strong Presbyterian, and the Presbyterians' Centre College in Danville in the border state of Kentucky had developed a strong academic reputation in the South. Lunsford enrolled for the February through June term.[21]

By early 1865, wartime had reduced Centre College's student body by more than half—to eighty-seven—and Lunsford Lewis was now the lone student from Virginia. He signed up in the Scientific Department, usually chosen by students not planning to stay four years for a degree, and took classes in mathematics, Greek, and Latin. He boarded with the family of a Danville businessman who happened to have roots in Rockingham's neighboring Augusta County. "The family here is *so kind*," he wrote brother Charles. "It almost seems as tho I were with relations." He also reported that, while socializing with Union Army personnel stationed nearby, a general had offered him a position as an officer on his staff. Lunsford politely declined.[22]

During his stay in Washington, Charles H. Lewis stayed in contact with Attorney General Edward Bates and with other Virginia expatriates, including Harrisonburg brothers Robert and Charles Gray and two children of

Unionist John Minor Botts. Beverley, Botts's son, was working in the Quartermaster Department while avoiding conscription. Daughter Rosalie had come with a neighbor to shop for necessities unavailable back in Culpeper County, and also with an unspecified request for President Lincoln. "I presented them to the president, who received them kindly," wrote Bates, "and granted their request."[23]

Charles H. Lewis went on to Alexandria, capital of the Restored Government of Virginia. The entity had been formed in 1861 by Unionist legislators, most from western Virginia, who refused to resign their seats and join the Confederate state government. The legislators—still the duly elected representatives of their constituents—fled Richmond to establish what they claimed was the state's true capital, safely in Unionist territory in farthest northwestern Virginia, in Wheeling. For the Reorganized—later Restored—Government of Virginia, the Unionists chose as governor Morgantown native Francis H. Pierpont. The Restored Government gave its permission to Virginia's northwestern counties to form their own state. The U.S. Congress declared the process valid and in June 1863 admitted West Virginia as the thirty-fifth state. With Wheeling no longer in Virginia, the Restored Government moved its capital to Alexandria, in northern Virginia across the Potomac from Washington and safely behind Union lines.[24]

Charles H. Lewis, with his Unionist credentials and numerous connections, met with a warm welcome in Alexandria. He was hired as an aide to Governor Pierpont at $100 a month. He began assuming duties of the Restored Government's original secretary of the commonwealth, Lucian A. Hagans, one of the two cabinet members who made the move from Wheeling to Alexandria and who was preparing to return to West Virginia. On April 1, Charles H. Lewis was formally appointed secretary of the commonwealth.[25]

In February 1865, Virginian Union Loyalist refugees had gathered in Alexandria to celebrate Washington's Birthday. They were addressed by Robert Gray, who left Harrisonburg with his family under Sheridan's protection four months earlier.

"Is this an assemblage of traitors?" Gray asked his listeners. "Are we traitors and cowards? We are represented as such in Dixie land today, and we have a right here to ask and answer that question.... From my earliest childhood to manhood I had been taught by those I considered good and wise to love and protect this Union, which I did. I told them that in their attempt to overthrow the government and destroy the Union I would not cooperate—and suddenly, in the brief space of a night, I found myself denounced because I would not help tear down the structure. I remained in my Valley home as

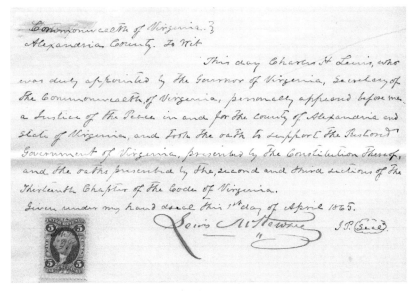

Charles H. Lewis is shown in a photograph taken in Virginia's Unionist capital of Alexandria. On April 1, 1865 he was appointed secretary of the commonwealth of the Restored Government of Virginia by its governor, Francis H. Pierpoint, who later dropped the second "i" in his last name to make it Pierpont. The oath of office was notarized by Lewis McKenzie, a Unionist mayor of Alexandria.

long as possible, suffering without complaint all the privations incident upon a state of war. I was so situated that both armies struck me, until all around was a scene of devastation, and the very landmarks had vanished. Their great principle was against coercion, and yet they undertook to force me to take up arms in a cause I did not approve, to destroy a government I did not wish to have destroyed. . . .

"That we are exiled from our old homes, banished forever, may depend upon circumstances. If they should succeed in breaking up this great Union and establish a grand slave-ocracy, with its Legrees and slave markets, its handcuffs, its tears and its blood, why, I'll perhaps not want to return. . . .

"But, my friends, I predict that we will return—you to the blackened walls of Fredericksburg, and you to the desolated shores of the Rappahannock and the James, whilst I, with others here, will turn our footsteps toward the green Valley, [and] look again with pleasure and delight into the homes of the Massanutten, as it casts its evening shadows upon the red waters of the Shenandoah."[26]

6

Moderates in the Postwar Tumult

Robert Gray's stirring address to Union Loyalist refugees in Alexandria did not win him many friends back home. Once it was published, Rockingham County's southern partisans became "greatly incensed against me," he recalled, and he was warned "I could never come back if the Confederates succeeded." Gray and his family went west to stay in Ohio. There he learned, only seven weeks after his speech in Alexandria, that Robert E. Lee had surrendered at Appomattox. Americans everywhere could echo Gray's emotional reaction upon hearing the news: "My feelings may be imagined, but not described."[1]

With the war over, refugees began returning home. On his way back, Robert Gray's brother Charles described parts of the Shenandoah Valley as "almost a desert," with "chimneys standing without houses and houses standing without roof or door or window." Barns were burned, bridges gone, roads torn up. Wheat grew in fields no longer protected by fences from roaming cattle, hogs, sheep, and horses. "Someone asked me whether the stock would destroy the wheat," Charles Gray recalled. "I said, 'Certainly, if General Sheridan had not taken the precaution of removing all the stock.' "[2]

Anne Lewis Walton did not return to Lynnwood. She had left the home, in disarray as a military hospital after the Battle of Port Republic, in the care of an uncle so she and her young daughters could join her Confederate chaplain husband, Robert Walton, in northern Georgia. Her husband had developed chronic respiratory problems, and the climate there seemed better suited to his health. They reluctantly decided to remain. Early in 1865, with expectations in the South that the war could go on much longer, Anne Walton sold Lynnwood to her first cousin John F. Lewis for $80,000 in Confederate securities. She later received additional compensation.[3]

Within two seasons, Samuel Hance Lewis, 71, had Lewiston flourishing once again. Crops of wheat, corn, and clover seed were planted and harvested with the aid of three of his former slaves—brothers Abram, Eugene, and Robert James—who had stayed on after emancipation. He helped revive the Episcopal Church's Rockingham Parish, which chose as its rector the Rev. Henry A. Wise Jr., former Confederate Army chaplain and namesake son of the onetime governor, the fiery secessionist who had been made a Confederate general.[4]

Not long after they returned, Lunsford and Daniel Sheffey Lewis enrolled in the law department of the University of Virginia. William M. Lewis, by nature so uncharacteristically "reticent" in the strongly opinionated family, resumed his life as a bachelor farmer, and rarely appears again in the historical record. Charles H. Lewis, who shepherded the three down the valley with Sheridan's army and became secretary of the commonwealth of the Restored Government of Virginia, stayed with his associates as they moved from Alexandria to Richmond, on May 25, to replace Virginia's Confederate government.[5]

In Richmond, Charles H. Lewis focused on bringing administrative order to the state and encouraging Congress to restore Virginia's full rights in the Union. President Andrew Johnson had been granting amnesties to former Confederates and favoring local autonomy in the South. But his desire for amnesty for so many former Confederates was running into trouble from a Congress dominated by radical Republicans, who sought more stringent terms. Less than three months after the Confederate surrender, Secretary of the Commonwealth Charles H. Lewis alerted the president that his friend John T. Harris, prewar Congressman from Rockingham County, was on his way to Washington to present Johnson with "a fair idea of the work before us." This would include evidence "that Virginia will be, henceforth, one of the most loyal States in the Union." Most Virginians "cheerfully acquiesce" in the ban against slavery, Lewis assured the president, and "shall be able to dispose of the vexed question" of enacting appropriate civil rights legislation for black freedmen "if the extreme radicals will but let us alone."[6]

Samuel Hance Lewis was a scarce commodity as an acceptable state appointee, for the Restored Government's constitution of 1864 banned from public office those who held any military or civil office in the Confederate government. Gov. Francis Pierpont appointed Lewis a board member of an entity named the Virginia Emigration and Land Company, headed by Pierpont—Charles H. Lewis was also a director—and intended to promote industry in the state. In June 1865 the governor also named Samuel Hance Lewis to the reorganized Board of Visitors of the University of Virginia.[7]

Once Mount Vernon Furnace was burned in September 1864 and its workers scattered, a clue to John F. Lewis's whereabouts for the rest of the war is a partial miscellaneous voucher headed "Lewis, Crawford & Co., Augusta Co., Va., Contractors" with the notation "Furnaces & Forges, Feb'y 15, 1865." One might conclude that he had gotten into special contract work with one of the furnaces or forges in neighboring Augusta County that had not been seriously damaged and thus kept his military service exemption through war's end.[8]

Though Mount Vernon Furnace's shops and buildings were burned by Union soldiers, there is no report that its stone stack was badly damaged—in which case, as with several other furnaces "burned" during the war, no major reconstruction was necessary. But any rebuilding would be a task for others. By the end of 1865, John F. Lewis and the other partners of Lewis, Crawford & Co. had sold Mount Vernon Furnace to Abbott Iron Company of Baltimore for $30,000, today's equivalent of $400,000. Ironmaster Manasseh Blackburn stayed on to help put the operation back in shape. Blackburn, who had moved down from Pennsylvania eight years before, soon found that good will from his hiring so many local workers for the furnace project reduced the hostility he previously felt for being one of the "Yankees and intruders and such things."[9]

Now that John F. Lewis's family was, apparently, more financially secure and had a gracious home, he could afford time to deal with some pent-up opinions. His stand at the secession convention in 1861 had put him in touch with like-minded politicians throughout the state. He had honed skills in maneuvering through precarious situations while sheltering political dissidents under the nose of a hostile government. Few native Virginians had a personal background that better fit the new definition of political correctness and thus had the potential to aid Virginia's postwar recovery. Within months after the war's end, John F. Lewis, 47, determined to become the U.S. representative for the Sixth Congressional District of Virginia.

He ran as a Republican, though independently, as the state party was disorganized and no Republicans were running that year in Virginia's other congressional districts. He was quick to attack the shortcomings of a government that barred participation of large numbers of the governed, based on their wartime service. In addition to the state ban against former Confederates holding office, Congress had decreed in 1862 that all federal officeholders must sign a test of loyalty called the ironclad oath, swearing that they had never voluntarily borne arms against the United States nor given any sort of voluntary support to a hostile government.

If elected, John F. Lewis promised to "exert myself to have everyone restored to all the political rights he enjoyed before the war. . . . I think that the most lenient and kind course that can be pursued towards the Southern people, consistently with the duty of the Government, will be best calculated to restore peace, prosperity and a fraternal feeling." A simple oath to support the constitution should suffice.[10]

The federal ban against office holding happened to apply, John F. Lewis frequently pointed out, to his opponent, Alexander Hugh Holmes Stuart of Staunton, 58. Stuart was running as a Conservative, the more proper designa-

tion of Democrat at the time "not being pleasing to many who had formerly been Whigs," as Lunsford Lewis later explained. Stuart was better known and had formidable credentials, gained as a Whig congressman and as secretary of the interior under Millard Fillmore. Like Lewis, Stuart had been a Unionist delegate to the secession convention, helpful for working with northerners in Congress—except that Stuart ultimately signed the secession ordinance and thus could not legally be seated. Declared John F. Lewis: "My competitor was a very good 'Union man,' until the Union needed his support." Stuart countered that Lewis could not be seated because he had manufactured iron for the Confederacy, which Lewis retorted that he had done only under duress.[11]

Within months after the war ended, John F. Lewis was running for Congress. This photograph, taken in Washington between 1860 and 1875, is attributed to Matthew Brady or his nephew, Levin Handy.

As the back-and-forth wore on, Lewis seemed to gain the edge on the point, causing the *Charlottesville Chronicle*, just before the election, to switch its endorsement to Lewis. But Virginia Conservatives won nearly all races handily. Alexander H. H. Stuart defeated John F. Lewis 4,653 to 2,194. Of the 130 elected legislators, only 4 were Republicans. Black freedmen throughout Virginia and the South, however, were not allowed to vote, and southern Unionists objected that the Congressional elections, at least, were invalid. They bombarded Washington with demands that those newly elected to Congress from the South should not be seated. It took the new Congress, convening in December 1865 with even more radical Republicans than before, less than an hour to agree. None from Virginia or the South was seated. The new Congress began plans began to investigate general conditions in the old Confederacy and to impose new requirements for Reconstruction.[12]

Regardless of the ban against former Confederates holding state office, Virginia voters elected a large number of Confederate veterans to the new legislature. The legislators elected former Confederate Congressman John B. Baldwin of Staunton as their speaker. Then they went about making it all legal by revoking the 1864 state constitution's provision prohibiting those who bore arms against the United States from holding state office in the first place.

Next, as Charles H. Lewis complained, came the removal of "every Union man who held office by Governor Pierpont's appointment whom the legislature could reach." Baldwin, brother-in-law of John F. Lewis's congressional opponent Alexander H. H. Stuart, led the charge against Charles H. Lewis, even though Charles H. Lewis had earlier endorsed Baldwin's application for a presidential pardon. Lewis was replaced as secretary of the commonwealth effective mid-January 1866, a year before his term was to expire. Pierpont kept him on as an aide. The state's auditor and treasurer were also removed, and a Pierpont nominee for a judgeship was rejected. John C. Underwood was told to resign the U.S. Senate post the Restored Government elected him to before the war ended.[13]

The house cleaning was among issues reported on by Charles H. Lewis at hearings of the Congressional Joint Committee on Reconstruction, formed to hear about conditions from residents throughout the South. Forty-nine Virginians were among those summoned to testify. They included seventeen Unionists—among them Charles H. Lewis, John F. Lewis, Charles Douglas Gray and John Minor Botts—plus seven freed blacks and some former Confederates, including John B. Baldwin and Robert E. Lee.[14]

Although both Lewises testified that Unionists in the state were safe from harm and that Virginians in general would not again attempt secession nor try to reinstitute slavery, they expressed disappointment in the attitudes of former Confederates who had returned to office. "I was one of those who took an active part, immediately after the surrender of General Lee, in getting pardons for these people," said John F. Lewis. "I believe, as a general thing, they have failed to comprehend or appreciate the magnanimity of the government shown toward them. . . A great number of persons who have received their pardons are now acting in a way that they would not have done if the pardons had been withheld a few months longer."[15]

Brother Charles recalled a conversation in his office in December 1865, while he was secretary of the commonwealth, with prewar governor Henry A. Wise, who believed that Unionists were being a good deal kinder to former Confederates than if the situation were reversed and Confederates had won. "If I had caught Governor Pierpoint or yourself whilst I was in command, I would have hanged you," Wise told Lewis, "notwithstanding my respect for the honesty which has no doubt influenced your conduct." Wise laughed that many who had taken the loyalty oath so they could receive pardons regarded it as a "mere custom-house oath," and had said, "with tears in their eyes, that they feel degraded at having taken it to save their property."[16]

This helped Charles H. Lewis distrust the sincerity of the oath-takers and make a general conclusion nearly a year after the end of the war: "The design of the politicians and of the disloyal press is, as far as possible, to create an alienation of feeling, and to inculcate a spirit of bitterness among the southern people against the north. My decided impression is that the politicians, and a portion of the clergy, and the disloyal press, are busily engaged in that attempt."[17]

In expressing its feelings, the "disloyal press" could be less restrained. In April 1866, Staunton's *Valley Virginian* reprinted an item from the *Richmond Enquirer* referring to "that miserable scoundrel Charles H. Lewis, ex-Secretary of the Commonwealth of Virginia." The immediate reason for his being not only "miserable" but also "despicable" was for allegedly having a conversation—said to have been overheard by "a most respectable gentleman of this city"—encouraging a black barber to celebrate the anniversary of the Confederate withdrawal from Richmond. Wondered the *Enquirer*—and, by extension, the *Valley Virginian*—about Lewis: "What is to be thought of so vile a monster?"[18]

In the postwar political and economic turmoil, "copperheads," northerners who earlier supported the Confederacy, were now aiding onetime Confederates. Former Confederates charged that Virginia and the rest of the South were also being victimized by a plague of "carpetbaggers," commonly defined as transplanted northern opportunists who supported Republicans, no matter that many soon called carpetbaggers were established citizens who happened to have moved from the North decades before the war.[19]

New immigrants from the north were actually very good for Virginia, contended John F. Lewis, flying yet again in the face of hard-line Conservatives. "I have as much contempt for what I consider a carpet-bagger as any man can have; but I do not consider every man who comes to Virginia a 'carpet-bagger,' " he wrote the *New York Times*. "The person who was so unfortunate as to be born outside Virginia, but who comes here to live, gives better evidence of his appreciation of the resources of the old State than we who were born upon her soil and who had no control over the matter.

"We want several hundred thousand 'carpet-baggers' to come and help (by their energy and capital) to make the genial climate and fertile soil of old Virginia produce as much as the frosty climate and sterile soil of New-England. When we grow wise, we will welcome every addition to our population from the honest and industrious classes of our Northern brethren, whether they vote the Republican or the Conservative ticket."[20]

John Minor Botts and his family in 1863 at Auburn in Culpeper County, where they lived after Botts was banished from Richmond for his hostile stance as a Union Loyalist. At right is son Beverley, who married Charlotte Lewis. Rosalie, at her mother's right, married Charlotte's brother Lunsford. Daughter Isabel married Daniel Sheffey Lewis. The fourth child, Mary, married a Lewis in-law, Walter Hoxsey.

To old guard Confederates, such heresy classified John F. Lewis as one of the "scalawags," unscrupulous native southerners trying to improve their lot by allying with carpetbaggers. Most partisans, however, did not stop to question whether otherwise respectable southerners were stereotyped as carpetbaggers or scalawags only because, unlike the commonly perceived run of such undesirables, they simply dissented from the majority. The generic terms suited the aggrieved, and accuracy of the definitions stood, little examined, for generations.[21]

In this topsy-turvy world, former Confederates were running Virginia's legislature, blacks were granted few rights, and white Republicans were still scorned by their neighbors. Yet it was becoming clear to moderates that backward-looking Conservatives' failure to acknowledge the changed world was counterproductive. The only way for Virginia to regain its place in the nation, moderates believed, was to deal with whatever Republicans in Washington happened to hold the power, however distasteful their radical policies might be. Emerging as a key "cooperator" was John Minor Botts, the onetime Whig congressman and intemperate Union Loyalist imprisoned in Richmond, then banished to sit out the war at his new home, Auburn, near Brandy Station in Culpeper County. Gruff and heavyset, with "the appearance of a well-fed bullfrog," Botts was elected chairman of a convention of Unconditional Unionists in Alexandria in May 1866.[22]

Ninety-four who arrived at the convention were recognized as delegates; eighty were northern Virginians from Alexandria and Fairfax and Frederick counties. The fourteen others included a handful from eastern Virginia and three from Rockingham County—Robert A. Gray, George K. Gilmer and John F. Lewis. After two days of debate, the convention endorsed a moderate Reconstruction plan advanced by John Minor Botts. It sought, among other goals, a free state school system open to all and voting privileges for wartime Unionists white and black—but not immediately for former Confederates. Those, the majority believed, should be given some sort of cooling-off period before they tried "accomplishing with votes what they have failed to accomplish with bayonets." A name was adopted for the group: the Union Republican Party of Virginia. Among those picked for the party's eleven-member state central committee were John Minor Botts and John F. Lewis.[23]

Delegates left no doubt as to how they felt about the recent war. In a message incendiary to former Confederates but certain to be welcomed by those in Washington who controlled Virginia's fate, delegates unanimously approved a closing resolution proposed by John F. Lewis:

> Resolved, That this convention returns its sincere thanks to the gallant soldiers and sailors of the Federal army for the heroic valor displayed by them in putting down or suppressing the recent unholy and unjustifiable rebellion, and especially do we return our thanks to all members of the Federal army and navy from this and other States recently in rebellion against the Federal government.[24]

Unsurprisingly, the proceedings gained positive reviews in the North and hostile ones throughout Virginia. In heavily conservative Augusta County, Staunton's *Valley Virginian* simply called any report on the convention "too stupid to publish."[25]

Soon after the Alexandria meeting, in June 1866, Congress passed the Fourteenth Amendment providing civil rights for blacks and submitted it to the states for ratification. The Virginia legislature rejected the amendment almost unanimously. But as radical Republicans tightened their grip, in March 1867 Congress passed Reconstruction laws requiring all southern states to adopt that amendment and also to acknowledge those rights in new state constitutions before the states could be readmitted to their seats in Congress. Finally, Congress gave up on Governor Pierpont's ability to bring the Virginia legislature into line and put the state's military commander, Gen. John M.

Schofield, in full charge of the state. Pierpont remained the civilian governor, subservient to Schofield and with sharply curtailed authority. The new Reconstruction program disqualified many former Confederates from holding office, and mandated blacks' right to vote and hold office. While John F. Lewis embraced the end of slavery, he believed blacks were ill prepared for the sudden right to vote, and had opposed granting the privilege immediately. Now there was no choice but to accept it.[26]

Injecting a vast number of black votes into the election process changed the political equation and offered an opportunity for practical Republicans to end Reconstruction. Between Virginia's newly enfranchised black voters and the large number of reactionary conservatives lay what Richard Lowe termed "a floating bloc of native white moderate voters." If these white moderates could compromise on some issues with black voters, they might achieve a majority that could pass a state constitution meeting Reconstruction requirements. John Minor Botts, with the support of Governor Pierpont, sought to bring a broad base of these moderates together with more radical Republicans and blacks to a meeting in Charlottesville on July 4. An appeal went out to all unconditional Unionists to attend.[27]

Some 300 Unionists and Republicans who had not compromised their views during the war signed Botts's call. Most of them, said Charles H. Lewis, were not newcomers but "old Union Whigs and land owners," and many were members of pre–Revolutionary War families. In florid prose that left little to the imagination, the signers asked "all others of like condition, as common sufferers, not to throw away this golden opportunity to rescue ourselves, our children and the State from the hands of those who have brought nothing but ruin, desolation, want and wretchedness upon the land." By organizing in Charlottesville, they agreed, "we may be prepared to enter into the contest soon to take place for political supremacy with those who have shown such absolute unfitness for a judicious exercise of the power with which for years past they have been clothed by a confiding, but deceived, people." Near the top of one petition, not far from the signatures of both Pierpont and Botts, were those of four Lewises from Rockingham County: John F., Charles H., and the Samuel Hances senior and junior.[28]

The elder Samuel Hance Lewis's signature was shaky, as his health was declining from cancer. Though still active, he was beginning to miss meetings of the Board of Visitors at the University of Virginia. Samuel H. Jr. moved his growing family into Lewiston to help out. Family marriage patterns were also changing, with choices perhaps more limited due to prejudice against Union Loyalists. Rather than gaining spouses from a variety of well-known families near and far, the four children and grandchildren

To the Unconditional Union Men of Virginia.

The time has arrived when it becomes necessary for the loyal men of the State who have been panting for freedom for the last six years, and praying for the day when, supported and sustained by the power of the National Government, they could with safety to their persons and property, rise in the majesty of their *right*, if not of their *might*, and assert their emancipation from the most oppressive and tyrannical despotism that ever ground into the earth, men who could lay claim to freedom as an inheritance.

What have we been for the last six years but the abject slaves, first to military despotism, and since to the equally odious despotism of the press, in the hands of our hard task-masters?

The banner of your country is now spread over you to afford the opportunity to meet and confer in safety for your own, and the common good of our beloved but misguided old State, and lead her once more into the paths of peace, prosperity and freedom.

We, the undersigned, citizens of the State, who here avow ourselves as *unconditional Union men*, and members of the great "*Republican Union party*" of the United States, call upon all others of like condition as common sufferers not to throw away this golden opportunity, to rescue ourselves, our children, and the State from the hands of those who have brought nothing but ruin, desolation, want and wretchedness upon the land—to meet us in counsel in Charlottesville on the 4th of July next, for the purpose of consultation and general organization throughout the State, and that we may be prepared to enter into the contest, soon to take place for political supremacy, with those who have shown such absolute unfitness for a judicious exercise of the power with which for years past they have been clothed by a confiding, but deceived, people. In this incipient step for organization, we feel that it is indispensable we should confine ourselves to those alone who, like ourselves, never of their own accord raised their arms or their voice against, or entertained a wish for, the destruction of their country.

Let all such come who can come, and let each one look to it that no county in the State shall be unrepresented, that all may share alike in the grand and glorious achievements of universal freedom.

Respectfully, yours,

Jos M Humphreys Richmond

F. H. Pierpoint

Jno F. Lewis, Rockingham

Alex River Albemarle

Jno M Botts

W. L. Mumford

Saml. H Lewis Sr Rockingham

A L Hendricks Russel Co

Franklin Stearns Henrico

W. S. Lucados Pr Gure

Ch H Lewis, Rockingham

Geo. K Gilmer "

Wm Y. Mallory Dinwiddie

John B Lowry Pittsylvania

John W Cobbs " "

Geo. W. Booker Henry Co.

S H Lewis Jr Rockingham

Peyton S. Coles Albemarle

W Storber

Howk Moss Amelia

Buckingham

D E Booker Campbell

L. H. Chandler

Wm Childrey Petersburg

C. S. Mills Richmond

A. G. McHenry Caroline

P F Boyle Richmond

John W Bulmer Kingsdam

N Davidson Richmond

J B Clinton Amelia Clk

H S Merrell "

Richard A Anderson Col'd

Jno H Graves Amelia

Alfred Anderson " "

Jno E Booker " "

R G Fitzgerald "

Saml R Seay " "

Richard Forrester "

W E Noble " "

J W Fowlkes " "

of Samuel Hance Lewis married in the six years following the Civil War all wed Republicans, three of them children of John Minor Botts. Lunsford Lewis, now out of law school, married Rosalie Botts and moved to Culpeper County as aide to his new father-in-law. His older sister Charlotte married son Beverley Botts. Nephew Daniel Sheffey Lewis married Botts's youngest daughter Isabel. All three couples named their first-born sons for John Minor Botts.[29]

Lunsford Lewis began meeting Republicans from throughout the state while working with Botts, but he would not be dealing with a Charlottesville convention. In a flurry of maneuvers that included consultations with leading Republicans down from the North, the meeting was rescheduled for August in Richmond. An alliance of radical and moderate factions of Virginia's Republican party, however, did not survive the session. The more radical Republicans—some northern-born whites but more black freedmen— believed blacks should have an immediate role in government and former Confederates should be excluded from leadership. Moderates were more lenient toward former Confederates. They believed that blacks as yet lacked the background for full participation in government and, for the moment at least, should remain as a class of agricultural laborers. It was a fracture similar to those beginning in other Republican parties throughout the South.[30]

To deal with the ultimate need for a new state constitution required under Reconstruction—one that must grant blacks the right to vote—the Virginia legislature scheduled a statewide referendum for a constitutional convention. The election for delegates came in October 1867. Rockingham moderate Republicans John F. Lewis and George K. Gilmer announced their candidacy for the county's two slots. They were opposed by Conservatives John C. Woodson and Jacob N. Liggett. Lewis and Gilmer each had the overwhelming support of Rockingham's blacks, who gave them 304 votes each and only 9 and 10 to Woodson and Liggett. Rockingham whites, however, gave Lewis and Gilmer less than 300 votes each and Woodson and Liggett more than 1,000. But the larger number of blacks in eastern Virginia was enough to swing the overall majority of convention delegates to Republicans, most in the party's radical wing. The radicals were unlikely to compromise sufficiently with Conservatives to produce a constitution the entire body of Virginia voters would approve.[31]

The petition shown on the facing page is one of several supporting a July 4, 1867 convention in Charlottesville to help end Reconstruction. Among Union Loyalists signing this one were Samuel Hance Lewis and three of his sons—Charles H., John F., and Samuel H. Jr.

Charles H. Lewis, still an aide to Governor Pierpont, sent a hopeful eight-page letter describing the situation to Henry Wilson, a key radical Republican senator from Massachusetts, who had been in Virginia earlier promoting an alliance between the party's two factions. "There is much that is unfortunate in our situation that can be remedied by prudence and good management, with the assistance of our earnest and judicious friends in Congress," Lewis wrote. "I have recently convened with intelligent and respectable colored men who are keenly alive to the exigencies of the situation. They all agree that we must do something, and that speedily, to bring about a reunion of all the Republican elements of our state. It is now every day becoming more apparent that the colored people are losing their confidence in the men who have misled them."[32]

The constitutional convention, controlled by the radical wing of the Republican Party, was under the presidency of federally appointed District Judge John C. Underwood. It did, in April 1868, approve the draft of a proposed constitution with required reforms. But, as the moderates feared, it included clauses that would still disenfranchise many former Confederates and require a loyalty oath that would bar most white Virginians from office. The military governor, Gen. John Schofield, aware of these volatile issues, postponed a statewide vote on ratifying the constitution. In addition, Schofield finally replaced Governor Pierpont, with whom he increasingly disagreed, with carpetbagger Henry H. Wells, a radical Republican.[33]

As the stalemate dragged on, Reconstruction requirements that all officeholders in unreconstructed states must swear they had not supported the Confederacy made it difficult for Schofield and his successor, Gen. George Stoneman, to fill more than half of Virginia's nearly 5,500 offices, for they had run out of unconditional Unionists. Charles H. Lewis, out of a job following Pierpont's dismissal as governor, went home with a military government appointment as commonwealth's attorney for Rockingham County. Sheffey Lewis, just out of law school, was given the same position for Orange County. His classmate and uncle Lunsford Lewis was appointed commonwealth's attorney for several northern Virginia counties, among them Culpeper and Fauquier.[34]

In spring 1869, the impasse finally began to loosen. Republicans, dominated by radicals, nominated Henry Wells for reelection as governor and J. D. Harris, a well-known black physician, for lieutenant governor. Moderate Republicans knew that most conservative whites would never vote for a ticket with a black man as number two. They seized the opportunity to woo conservatives and formed their own party, the True Republicans. In their platform they included a promise to support the required black suffrage but also a vow to reject the radical Republicans' strictures disenfranchising former Confederates, who would be able to hold office once again.[35]

For governor the True Republicans nominated Gilbert C. Walker, a moderate carpetbagger and prominent businessman with important connections in Washington; for lieutenant governor, John F. Lewis, a native moderate with strong Unionist credentials acceptable to congressional Republicans. Charles H. Lewis was among the True Republican leaders who signed the formal announcement of the slate in March 1869. Conservatives so feared a radical Republican victory that the party did not nominate a state ticket, preferring instead to free its own moderates to support the True Republicans.[36]

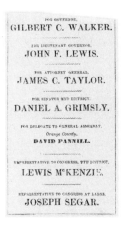

John F. Lewis briefly planned a run for Congress while also a candidate for lieutenant governor. In 1869, he issued a broadside, left, outlining his views. He dropped his Congressional candidacy, and was elected lieutenant governor.

The political ticket above was printed and distributed to support Republican candidates voted on in the election of 1869 in Orange County.

During the campaign, "one of the hardest fought in Virginia history," John F. Lewis declared his support for the president: "I am a Grant Republican, believing it is his earnest desire to see our 'bleeding country raised from the dust and set free.' I am convinced that the Republican Party can most surely and speedily accomplish this."[37]

John F. Lewis became so focused on his potential effectiveness in Washington that, a month before the election, he toyed with the idea of a concurrent campaign for Congress, for the same seat he had sought four years before. "My duties as Lieutenant-Governor will be merely nominal," he wrote in announcing his simultaneous congressional candidacy to Sixth District voters in early June 1869. Once elected lieutenant governor, he could organize the state senate and then resign "without detriment to the interest of Virginia." He would prefer representing the Sixth District to continuing as lieutenant governor, he explained, "because I believe I can have more influence with the dominant party in Congress than any man who can be elected and admitted to his seat." A week later, however, he withdrew from the congressional race.[38]

On July 6, in a turnout of 87 percent of Virginia voters, Gilbert C. Walker was elected governor with 54 percent, 119,535 to 101,204. John F. Lewis became lieutenant governor with 55 percent, 120,068 to 99,400. Reconstruction authorities gave approval for a vote, too, on the Underwood constitution, but with its controversial disenfranchise clause and test oath—included by the radical Republicans—stripped away, to be voted on as separate items. With those items removed, the constitution was approved, and the disenfranchise clause and test oath were defeated by large margins.[39]

With a state constitution acceptable to Congress at last ratified, the new legislature convened to ratify the Fourteenth and now the Fifteenth amendments to the U.S. Constitution, granting blacks full citizenship and the right to vote. All Reconstruction requirements now fulfilled, the U.S. House and Senate approved Virginia's restoration to its prewar status in the Union. The enabling bill was signed by President Grant on January 26, 1870. For Virginia, Reconstruction was over.

But John F. Lewis's recent brief candidacy for Congress seems to have made his point with party leaders. Shortly after the newly elected legislature was seated, Lt. Gov. John F. Lewis was sent to Washington as U.S. senator, in the days before the Seventeenth Amendment changed choice of senators to direct popular election. His Union Loyalist background was balanced by that of Virginia's other new senator, Abingdon lawyer John W. Johnston, a onetime minor Confederate government official. Johnston became the first former backer of the Confederacy to serve in the U.S. Senate.

On election day, July 6, 1869, Samuel Hance Lewis was bedridden with hardly a month to live. Yet he insisted on being carried the two miles from Lewiston to the polls in Port Republic so he could vote for the Walker–Lewis ticket. He lived long enough to know that the election results assured that his beloved state could return to its old status in the Union, and that his founding forebears' principles he had so firmly passed on to his children would endure—and be championed, no less, by a son now vindicated and elected to high office.[40]

John Minor Botts had died six months earlier. His daughter Rosalie and her young husband and his aide, Lunsford Lewis, stayed on in Culpeper County.[41]

An improbable locale awaited oldest son Charles H. Lewis, so unceremoniously thrown out as secretary of the commonwealth in Richmond a few years before. President Ulysses S. Grant rewarded him—on March 1, 1870—with appointment as U.S. Minister Resident to Portugal. It was one of thirty-five nations with high U.S. diplomatic posts and important to the Navy's use of ports of call in remnants of the Portuguese Empire. He arrived in Lisbon on June 5.[42]

Scarcely a month after Reconstruction ended in Virginia, Charles H. Lewis was preparing to leave for Lisbon as the new U.S. minister resident to Portugal.

Ten days later, Charles Hance Lewis rode to the sprawling hilltop palace overlooking the city. He was escorted up its central staircase to an anteroom, adorned with royal tapestries, in the southern tower. At 1 p.m. he was ushered into the audience chamber. Aubusson carpets were spread over the parquet floor, walls were draped in red silk, and an immense bronze and crystal chandelier hung above. Amid the splendor, he wrote, "the King, in full uniform, was surrounded by the members of his cabinet, the counsellors of state, the chiefs of the Army and Navy, the officers of the palace and the gentlemen of the royal household, all in full court dress. His Majesty stood in front of the throne."

Luís I—By the Grace of God, and by the Constitution of the Monarchy, King of Portugal and the Algarves, of either side of the sea in Africa, Lord of Guinea and of Conquest, Navigation and Commerce of Ethiopia, Arabia, Persia and India—received the new minister's credentials, and responded.

"Immediately after the King had concluded," wrote Charles H. Lewis, "he left his position near the throne and advanced towards me. The King [grasped] me cordially by the hand. He expressed in the best of English (which he speaks fluently) the pleasure which he not only had in seeing me, but, also, he was glad of the opportunity to say to me, that it might reach the President of the United States, how great was his admiration personally for the Chief Magistrate of the Union."[43]

For the erstwhile lawyer, editor, poet and politician, and for the rest of the Lewis family, the previous ten years framed a remarkable journey indeed.

Epilogue: To a New Century

The worst may have seemed over for Virginia, but its crises did not end with Reconstruction. Finding financing to fix the war-damaged infrastructure despite massive state debt soon became even harder, thanks to a national depression. The two political parties began fracturing over how to pay the bills. Acrimony escalated into more shooting, this in a relict series of duels that drew national amazement. Charles H. Lewis had graduated to international diplomacy in Lisbon, but younger brothers John F. and Lunsford stayed in the thick of things at home, thrusting and parrying through the politics of the coming decades with some success until, finally, their rivals, the conservatives, turned Virginia into the one-party state it remained past the middle of the twentieth century.

But first, for many Union Loyalists, came a bit of unfinished housekeeping. Rockingham County's Confederacy supporters had kept careful track of their losses during Sheridan's campaign, expecting compensation from the state or Confederate government. They were out of luck. But many whose losses were due to the Union Army were not, as long as they could prove both their claims and unbending loyalty to the Union. That would be decided by the Southern Claims Commission, created by Congress in March 1871. When the commission's work ended nine years later, it had heard 22,298 cases claiming $60.3 million in damages, the present equivalent of more than $830 million. One authority blames "intense, minute and often absurdly rigid investigation and qualifying tests" for the approval of less than a third of the claims, with total payment of only $4.6 million.[1]

The claims and helping with pardons for those accused of supporting the Confederacy provided fertile fields for lawyers. Attorney Lunsford L. Lewis, 25, still in Culpeper, balanced his Union Loyalist background by going into practice with a Lewis third cousin, James Cochran, 41, a Confederate colonel who had commanded the 14th Virginia Cavalry. Among claims pursued by the firm of Cochran and Lewis was that of the Samuel H. Lewis estate, for the 600 bushels of corn taken on the eve of the Battle of Port Republic. At a value then of $600, the corn would have a present-day worth of more than $13,000.[2]

An envelope with postage waived by John F. Lewis's signature as U.S. Senator reflects the contact he maintained with his brother Lunsford, an attorney with whom he collaborated on pursuing pardons and Union Loyalist claims from the Civil War.

The estate's claim was filed in January 1872 and heard six years later in Richmond by two commissioners. John F. and Lunsford Lewis, coexecutors, testified to the loyalty of their father and of his heirs. Backing them up was testimony from longtime friend and political associate George K. Gilmer; Union Loyalist E. J. Sullivan, Harrisonburg postmaster; and Abram James, a former family slave. Of the eight surviving children and heirs, however, son William M. Lewis was ruled disloyal due to his service in the Confederate Army. Commissioners reduced the amount of the claim by one-eighth and—in July 1880—finally paid the balance, $525.[3]

Claims rulings, however, were often arbitrary. While the estate decision visited the perceived sins of son William on the father, the commissioners gave son Samuel H. Jr. a pass, even though different commissioners ruling on an earlier claim had found him wanting. That claim sought $440 for two horses and 1,000 feet of fence rails taken at the time of the Battle of Port Republic. In disallowing that claim, in 1875, commissioners agreed with witnesses that "there is much in the evidence . . . to show that he was loyal" and that in his early service in the Virginia militia and as a justice of the peace in the Confederate county government "he did these acts unwillingly. But there seems to be no sufficient proof of duress, and we are obliged to find the loyalty not proved." A joint claim by Manasseh Blackburn and John F. Lewis for losses at Mount Vernon Furnace totaling $3,204—now about $44,000—was allowed.[4]

In Washington, Sen. John F. Lewis was being "as quiet and unassuming in the Senate as he had been in the secession convention." He was chairman of the Committee on the District of Columbia and author of a bankruptcy law, but he got headlines for using his access to the White House to make a sensational political connection. John Singleton Mosby, the Confederate cavalry hero legendary as the Gray Ghost, had opposed Reconstruction as backed by radical Republicans and instead supported the Walker–Lewis ticket. In early 1872 he wanted to carry this a step further and endorse the reelection of U. S. Grant. The president was opposed by abolitionist newspaper editor Horace Greeley, a former Whig and Republican who was trying, as a Democrat, to appeal to the southern elite. Mosby asked Senator Lewis to introduce him to Grant. The introduction occurred in the White House, and the meeting of the wartime adversaries brought national attention. Southerners who considered Grant "a threat to civilization" were shocked. Mosby endured the political storm, and the endorsement aided his newfound friend Grant in carrying Virginia while being reelected.[5]

John F. Lewis had a brush with higher office at the same time. At the Republican convention in Philadelphia in June 1872, Grant had no difficulty being renominated for president, though his vice president, Schuyler Colfax Jr., faced a strong renomination challenge from Massachusetts senator Henry Wilson. Since Reconstruction was ending in the South, delegates from three Southern states thought it a fine opportunity to display national unity by having a nominee from the South as vice president. Tennessee delegates thought it should be one of their state's congressmen, Horace Maynard. Texas delegates preferred their governor, Edmund J. Davis. Virginia delegates nominated Sen. John F. Lewis. None of those nominees, however, attracted more than two votes beyond their home state delegations. Virginia delegates were the first to break, as twenty of the state's twenty-two delegates switched their support to Henry Wilson, an old friend of Virginia Republicans. That put Wilson within a few votes of the 377 needed for nomination. Others quickly followed, and Wilson ultimately became the next vice president.[6]

Meanwhile, in Lisbon, Minister Resident Charles H. Lewis was keeping an eye on Portuguese politics, working on a trade treaty, seeking to suppress illegal emigration of unskilled Chinese workers through Macao, assessing whether an uprising in Spain might spill across the border, and staying attentive to the U.S. Navy's use of strategic harbors in Portugal and its far-flung possessions. When the Navy's Mediterranean Squadron happened to be visiting Lisbon during the birthday of the queen, Lewis arranged for Admiral James Alden to host a reception on board the flagship frigate USS *Wabash* for the royal couple, who were "entertained in a manner appropriate to the occasion." The king—an admiral himself before ascending the throne—in turn invited Admiral Alden and his captains to dinner at the royal palace. All told, Minister Lewis reported to the State Department, "the visit of the fleet has strengthened the favorable sentiment entertained here in regard to our country."[7]

When not so engaged, Charles H. Lewis could enjoy the Lisbon scene. "Quiet reigns in the city now," he wrote a sister-in-law after Mardi Gras in March 1871, "a striking contrast to the 'noise and confusion' of the carnival. During the three days preceding Ash Wednesday, the streets were thronged with hilarious & noisy groups, many of them in masquerade dresses of the most grotesque description, pelting each other with sugar plums, oranges & eggshells filled with flour, and playing all manner of practical jokes. I walked out several times to see the sights, which I could do without risk of being covered with sugar or flour, as the persons of ministers are, on such occasions, respected as usual." He shipped wine and silks back to Virginia, and kept up a correspondence with his nieces and nephews.[8]

Five years after his initial welcome at the royal palace in Lisbon, Charles H. Lewis bade farewell at a similar reception there on April 8, 1875. After two months of travel in Europe, he retired to Rockingham County. He began a history of Portugal, though his papers were lost when his home was flooded by the Shenandoah River, and he did not resume work. He died of cancer in May 1880, at 64.[9]

John F. Lewis left the Senate in 1875, at the end of his term. Two years earlier, he had informed the Republican Party that he would not be a candidate for governor. The marriage of convenience between Republicans and Conservatives that helped Virginia back to its status as a full-fledged member of the Union was fracturing, and in 1873 Conservatives had taken the statehouse away from the True Republicans. John F. Lewis went back to Lynnwood with an appointment from President Grant as U.S. marshal for the Western District of Virginia, renewed in 1878 by President Rutherford B. Hayes.[10]

An economic alarm brought the Lewis family back into the political majority. The Panic of 1873 kicked off a lengthy national depression made worse in Virginia by a per capita public debt more than twice the national average. State budgets ran major deficits. Slashing expenses and raising taxes were of little help. Virginia's $45 million debt, more than $1 billion in today's dollars, almost entirely predated the war. It stemmed from $30 million in railroad construction and other internal improvements and had grown by more than half due to unpaid interest. Much of that work had been destroyed during the war, and some, following creation of West Virginia, was no longer even in the state. New money had to be found.[11]

Conservatives and Republicans reshuffled into two new factions over a solution. Many old-line Conservatives saw growth as a gradual process and, committed to paying bills whatever the consequences, became known as Funders. Those who believed the situation called for reform were named Readjusters. They organized into a political party in 1879 under former Conservative Party leader William Mahone, railroad magnate and a prime supporter of the Walker–Lewis ticket a decade earlier. The Readuster Party rallied the disaffected—"the yeomen, the blacks, the new middle class"—and urged that the state's

An economic crisis in Virginia brought John F. Lewis election as lieutenant governor a second time, in 1881.

economy be jump-started by "readjusting" the debt downward by a third, then placing a much lower interest rate on the remainder.[12]

At first Virginia Republicans in convention outvoted party moderates by disapproving readjustment. Moderate John F. Lewis was elected party chairman to placate the minority. But when Republicans badly lost the 1880 election, John F. Lewis blamed party managers for fumbling the campaign, and led many fellow Republicans into a coalition with the Readjuster Party. Readjusters nominated Petersburg Mayor William E. Cameron for governor and John F. Lewis for lieutenant governor. In a hard-fought campaign, the Cameron–Lewis ticket was elected in November 1881.[13]

An indication of how seriously Virginians were taking debt payment was the sudden resurgence of an old method of conflict resolution, the code duello, often observed within the southern aristocracy before the war. Though duels had since been outlawed, bitter disputes over the debt crisis took prominent Virginians to the dueling field on six occasions, gaining national attention.[14]

In election campaign remarks in September 1881, Congressman George D. Wise, outspoken nephew of the equally outspoken prewar Democratic

Gov. Henry A. Wise, attacked the personal integrity of Readjuster candidates, including John F. Lewis. His brother Lunsford Lewis, infuriated, responded during a campaign speech in Petersburg that Wise was "a liar, a scoundrel and a fool." His comments, like Wise's, were picked up in the press. Wise's brother Peyton wrote the *Richmond Daily Dispatch* to denounce both Lunsford Lewis and his brother in what the *New York Times* thought "the severest possible language." Not only was Lunsford Lewis a "liar," a "coward," and a "fool," he was also a "blackguard." And John F. Lewis was no better. According to the code of honor, noted the *Times*, the severity of the language did "not admit of an amicable settlement." Lunsford Lewis challenged Peyton Wise to a duel.[15]

It was supposed to be pistols at ten paces in Washington, D.C. on September 19. But with the nation's newspapers already predicting the precise location, the risk of police surveillance was deemed too great. That night Wise slipped out of town in a carriage and boarded a train to nearby Warrenton, Virginia. Lewis followed early the next morning, in disguise. On the field in Warrenton, Lunsford Lewis, unfamiliar with his weapon, took aim, but missed his target. Wise intentionally fired his pistol into the air. The opponents called themselves satisfied. One historian noted that had Peyton's Congressman brother George, whose intemperate comments started the affray, been able to reach the site of the duel in time to take Peyton's place, the outcome could have been quite different.[16]

Three other members of the Lewis family were involved nearly two years later—in June 1883—in Virginia's last major duel. It followed an exchange of insulting editorials between Richard F. Beirne, editor of the *Richmond State*, and William C. Elam, editor of the *Richmond Whig* and secretary of the commonwealth in the Readjuster administration. As soon as he heard of Elam's latest editorial, Richmond's mayor, who knew that the two had already been involved in dueling incidents, issued warrants for their arrest for being "about to engage in a duel." But Beirne had already issued the challenge, Elam had accepted, and neither could be found.[17]

The duel, anxiously anticipated in the national press, was about to begin near Hanover Junction on June 20, when a sheriff appeared and arrested Beirne. Elam fled, and Beirne soon escaped from his captor. The two reappeared ten days later at sunrise on a Shenandoah Valley farm near Waynesboro. Although John F. Lewis had been kept unaware of the proceedings, Elam's retinue included two of the lieutenant governor's sons and a nephew: Sheffey Lewis, Elam's second; John F. Lewis Jr.; and Dr. Samuel Hance Lewis Wheat of Richmond, Elam's physician. Navy revolvers had been purchased, and the number of paces was shortened from ten to eight due to Elam's nearsightedness. In the first round, both adversaries missed. In the second, Elam's shot went over Beirne's head and Beirne's went into Elam's thigh, ending the duel. Elam was carried twenty-two miles north to Lynnwood, John F. Lewis's home. Visiting grandson Minor Botts Lewis, 13, brushed away flies while Dr. Wheat removed the bullet, without benefit of anesthetic.[18]

Dueling may have been dangerous and illegal, but it was not necessarily hazardous to one's career. In summer 1882, Readjuster Governor William Cameron—himself wounded in a politically inspired duel in 1869—appointed Lunsford Lewis to a vacancy on the Supreme Court of Appeals of Virginia, later known as the Supreme Court of Virginia. At the beginning of the 1883 term, members of the court elected him president—now chief justice. "Independent and fearless" as he was, noted a later tribute, Lunsford Lewis promptly became the lone dissenter in a 4–1 decision that favored a prominent Readjuster. By the time he left the bench in 1894, the court over which Judge Lewis presided had decided 1,446 cases. He had delivered the majority opinion in 407.[19]

As state and nation recovered a degree of prosperity, the debt crisis became less critical, and those Conservatives and Republicans who had united as Readjusters fell to quarreling. Readjuster majorities declined sharply, and in November 1883 the party lost control of the legislature. Social conservatives emphasizing the issue of "white supremacy" over feared "Negro rule" coalesced into the Democratic Party and became dominant once again. The Readjuster Party collapsed. Many former members returned to the Republican Party. When his term as lieutenant governor expired in 1886, John F. Lewis went back to Lynnwood. He grew disenchanted with the "Bossism" of his longtime Republican ally William Mahone and in 1889 broke with the slightly built Mahone, whom he disparaged as "the little villain." Soon John F. Lewis was writing George K. Gilmer, "I am glad you have faith in the administration. Hope on, brother. I am a 'Thomasite,' and feel very little interest in politicks, and very great disgust for politicians." He had already complained that there were too many "mercenary Republicans" interested in fighting only for what yielded them personal financial gain. Eventually, he feared, that would drive away altruistic Republicans "until there is only enough left of the party to hold the Federal offices."[20]

Appointments to federal offices in Virginia indeed began providing Republicans with their only dependable toeholds in the state, as long as there was a Republican administration in Washington to make the appointments. John F. Lewis, appointed U.S. marshal between his term as senator and his second election as lieutenant governor, went not only to the postmaster general but also to President Hayes himself to assure that his longtime friend George Gilmer would be named postmaster of Richmond. His oldest son, Daniel Sheffey Lewis, whose Republican bona fides included an unsuccessful run for Congress in 1876, served four years as U.S. attorney for the West-

ern District of Virginia, until removed in 1886 by Hayes's Democratic successor, Grover Cleveland. He then managed to be elected the first Republican mayor of Harrisonburg—a feat the *New York Times* found worthy of mention—and purchased a local newspaper, *Spirit of the Valley*. Sheffey's Republican brother-in-law Beverley Botts was also in Harrisonburg, with an appointment as U.S. internal revenue collector for the Western District of Virginia.[21]

Before their party fell apart, Readjusters had broadened their platform to back such "liberal" reforms as railroad regulation, federal aid to mining and manufacturing, and repeal of the poll tax burdening black voters. They could claim at least some credit for a commercial boom, even though their debt reduction plan was struck down by the

Daniel Sheffey Lewis, eldest son of John F. Lewis, made an unsuccessful run for Congress as a Republican in 1876 and later owned a Harrisonburg newspaper.

U.S. Supreme Court in 1885. Seven years after that, Democrats and creditors agreed on more extended terms, and the debt matter was settled. James Tice Moore found the era "one of the most eventful periods in Virginia's history. . . . Abandoning the solid South, for a time, at least, the state had experienced real two-party competition." But once "the mass of white voters relapsed into their normal conservatism," Virginia, he sensed, drifted back into limbo, "suspended between the lost antebellum world and the industrial promise of the future."[22]

A last political hurrah for the Lewises—and a final all-out challenge to establishment Democrats from the era's Virginia Republicans—came under the banner of Lunsford Lewis. In Culpeper County, Lunsford Lewis held his 1873 appointment as U.S. attorney for the Eastern District of Virginia until he moved to Richmond to serve on the Supreme Court, in 1882. After thirteen years on the bench he began a law practice in Richmond, and the next year—1896—ran unsuccessfully for Congress as a Republican. President

Theodore Roosevelt on occasion sought his opinion and apparently was sufficiently pleased to appoint Lunsford Lewis, 56, again as U.S. attorney for the Eastern District of Virginia. Three years later, in 1905, he resigned to run for governor. A Republican had not held that office since Gilbert Walker's term expired in 1874.[23]

It would be an uphill battle, for Republicans counted on votes from blacks, and in 1902 a Democratic-revised state constitution had limited the ability of blacks to vote. Nevertheless, Republicans mounted a full-court press, and hoped to gain a boost from the popularity of the national Roosevelt Republican administration. The party's convention was held in Roanoke, a Republican stronghold in southwestern Virginia. The proposed ticket was nominated without opposition. Lunsford Lewis's nomination for governor was seconded by one of the few black delegates, W. H. C. Brown, who was careful to reassure white voters that blacks need not be feared, that they wished only, as the *Roanoke Times* reported, to emulate "the civilization of the whites and [follow] at a respectable distance."[24]

After Lunsford Lewis's unsuccessful 1905 candidacy for governor, supported by black voters, Virginia Republicans languished until finally retaking the statehouse in 1970, during the civil rights movement.

Republicans, however, were swamped. Seven-term Democratic Congressman Claude A. Swanson, 43, was elected governor with 83,544 votes to Lewis's 45,975. Republicans had scarcely a third of the total, well down from the forty-one percent they tallied in the previous election. It marked "a major turning point in Virginia politics," writes Raymond Pulley. "Those who ascribed to the traditionalist leadership values and goals were left in unchallenged control, [establishing] once and for all that Virginia would be governed according to the rules and standards set down in the Old Virginia mystique."[25]

It would be another sixty-five years before Republicans could move back into the Virginia statehouse—in 1970, when the national civil rights movement and drive for racially integrated schools had reenergized the party's historic base of blacks, small farmers and working class voters. The new governor—A. Linwood Holton Jr., a white native of southwestern Virginia—made front pages of newspapers throughout the country when he escorted his daughter into a nearly all-black high school in Richmond.[26]

Lunsford Lewis and his kin may have been ahead of their time in Virginia in dealing with equal rights, but they had also demonstrated that finer elements of the "Old Virginia mystique" were not the exclusive property of

Lunsford Lomax Lewis, whose legal career included twelve years as chief justice of Virginia's Supreme Court, was the last surviving member of his family's generation of Union Loyalists.

traditionalists of Democratic or ultra-conservative persuasion. After his defeat in 1905 Lunsford Lewis went back to private law practice, and to a third appointment (1910–12) as U.S. attorney. When he died in 1920 at 73, a Richmond newspaper observed that "in his private life he was the cultured, unassuming gentleman, the Virginian of the old school, a type that has all but passed away."[27]

In the evolving scene along the Shenandoah, Lewiston had burned in 1875, and was rebuilt. Eleven years later, Samuel H. Lewis Jr. and his family moved from Lewiston across to their new home, Mapleton, on a hillside above the old coaling. His sister Elizabeth moved into Lewiston with her husband, the Rev. Dr. James C. Wheat, newly retired headmaster of an Episcopal girls' school in Winchester. Across from Lewiston, a small Episcopal church was built in a ravine on the site of the heaviest fighting in the Battle of Port Republic, and named Grace Memorial in memory of those killed in the battle. Windows above the altar are in memory of Elizabeth Wheat's father, Samuel Hance Lewis.[28]

James C. Wheat, in retirement the church's first rector, assisted daughter Eleanor in setting up Lewiston Home School for Girls, which occupied the house for more than two decades. The long-awaited Shenandoah Valley Railroad, later part of the Norfolk & Western, extended a rail siding to the family mill. The mill also housed the Lynnwood post office, as the community took on the name of that home. The Lynnwood depot was first known as Lewis Station.[29]

John F. Lewis, done with politics, sold the mill and concentrated on operating Lynnwood as a stock breeding farm for thoroughbreds and registered saddle horses. Son John F. Jr. added breeding of Percheron draft horses, ideal for heavy hauling. Soon John F. Lewis became ill with cancer and began a painful decline of five years. At the time of his death in 1895, at 77, he was described in the *New York Times* as "of a warm and generous nature, brave, magnanimous and outspoken, and intensely loyal to his friends." The newspaper ran his likeness, and described a multitude of accomplishments.[30]

Some two decades after the Civil War, a granddaughter of Samuel Hance Lewis operated a school for girls at Lewiston. This photo, taken in about 1910, shows the home remodeled with windows added on either side of the chimney.

But a visiting niece twenty years before had already found him "talking very sensibly and seriously about the worthlessness of worldly honors,"[31] and it is the record of only a solitary stand of heartfelt defiance that is chiseled into the granite obelisk that rises in the center of the family cemetery at Lynnwood:

JOHN F. LEWIS
Voted against and refused to
sign Ordinance of Secession
in Va. Convention 1861, inflexibly
believing in the Union, the
Constitution and the enforcement
of the laws.

Acknowledgments

In one sense, this book has been in the works for more than fifty years. Thus many of my acknowledgments must be to persons no longer living.

It was an eerie feeling lately to be up from Texas doing research in Virginia for this book and come face-to-face—twice—with copies of my high school senior term paper, written so long before in upstate New York. The subject was the Battle of Port Republic, fought in 1862 around the Shenandoah Valley birthplace of my grandfather, who died when I was nine. The offer of my history teacher, Charles G. Rose, to give extra class credit to seniors who did their English class research paper on a historical subject clicked with news of the approaching centennial of the Civil War. How my grandfather's Union Loyalist family managed when their home was in the midst of one of Confederate Gen. Stonewall Jackson's great victories seemed a promising topic to look into.

My grandfather, Charles Thomas Lewis, left Virginia for upstate New York soon after 1900 for a job advancing the new technology of telephones. He became a Southwestern Bell district manager in southeastern Kansas. New friends were always surprised that he, a Virginian, was yet a Republican. He and my grandmother retired back to her homeland near Rochester. After his death in 1951, the memory of his gentlemanly manner and a soft accent that seemed so out of place made me curious about his origins.

I found some answers a few years later, when my parents, J. Sheldon and Lillian Lewis Fisher, took our family on an a trip through the Virginias, visiting relatives and historic sites. My grandmother, Katharine Fairchild Lewis, had carefully preserved my grandfather's few family papers and photographs. Being some distance from relatives with more information, as I undertook the term paper I found myself writing members of his generation I had met with the sort of questions usually thought of only when it's too late. They were delighted to answer. With long distance calls then expensive and email nowhere in sight, they responded in letters, most helpful for the historical record.

My grandfather's first cousin Minor Botts Lewis, retired publisher of the *Clifton Forge Daily Review* and grandson of two prominent Union Loyalists—

John Minor Botts and John F. Lewis—put me in touch, months before his death at 88, with a second cousin near Philadelphia, Anne Mays Miller, who died a few years later. Her grandmother, Anne Lewis Walton, had fled her home as the Battle of Port Republic was imminent. Anne Miller turned to a Florida cousin on another side, Lillian McFarland, to produce a transcript from a diary kept in 1862 by Lillian's Richmond grandmother, Lucy Muse Walton Fletcher. In her diary, Lucy Fletcher quoted letters from her sister-in-law Anne Lewis Walton, relating her experiences at the time of the battle. Lucy Walton Fletcher's papers and her diary from 1864 to 1865 are now in the special collections at Duke University and are widely quoted for their insights on women during the Civil War. Her 1862 diary that I had indirect access to in the late 1950s is nowhere to be found.

My grandfather's youngest sister, Susan Lewis Durkee, provided information about the family of their father, Samuel Hance Lewis Jr. Her sister-in-law, my great-aunt Agnes Moses Lewis, lived on the battlefield and helped me obtain background from Charles E. Baker, last miller at the nearby mill, spared by Sheridan's army. When preparing to sell the home her father built, Aunt Sue mailed me a shoebox stuffed with documents found on top of a wardrobe and dating from the early nineteenth century. They yielded a wide range of details for this book that would otherwise have been lost.

Fast forward to 1985, when I did a good deed for a very distant cousin in California, Irvin Frazier, and put his *The Family of John Lewis, Pioneer* into shape for printing. To lift that book above the level of a plain family genealogy, he connected me with a third cousin of mine, Mark W. Cowell Jr., a lexicographer then living in New York. Mark had been doing family research as careful as one would imagine a lexicographer's to be. For the book he produced seven chapters that proved to be the most thorough and clear-headed of all the voluminous accounts about the earliest members of our family of Lewises in Virginia. He also began sending me a variety of obscure references that ended up being quite useful for this book.

Four years later, I was preparing for a newspaper meeting in Washington, D.C. and saw myself having a spare afternoon. On a hunch, I made an appointment at the National Archives with its Civil War specialist, Michael Musick—soon to be a consultant for the PBS television series *The Civil War* by Ken Burns—to see if there were on file any of the family claims supposedly made for caring for wounded soldiers after the Battle of Port Republic. When I arrived, I was cleared through an unmarked door and made the trek alone over a winding catwalk, beneath the glare of warehouse lighting and past locked cages securing tiers of shelved document boxes, until I reached Michael Musick's windowless aerie. There staff members spread before me several dozen pages of claims and depositions—the sworn testimony of members of my grandfather's family, their neighbors, even a slave, not for medical claims but for property losses. Witnesses testified of their wartime experiences with a frankness they would never have used with the general public, perhaps not even with close family.

It did not take me long to realize I had stumbled on to a story that transcended simple family history. It was a story I hoped someone else would write.

Another decade or so passed. Then Maurice Wyatt, a second cousin I had met only once, tracked me down from North Carolina. He had been clearing out a storage unit, found a few family items and wanted them in a safer place. What he sent me included apparently the only surviving images of patriarch Samuel Hance Lewis and of his oldest son, Charles H. Lewis. With key illustrations suddenly in hand, I knew it was indeed time for a book. But if I were to do it, I needed a big nudge. That finally came in January 2010 from a third cousin from Richmond, Richard H. Dilworth, who stopped by with his wife, Joan, to stay with Mary and me in San Antonio. Dick is a retired banker and knows how to persuade. By the time they left, he had me ready to start on this book.

A few months later, Mary and I went up to visit the Dilworths, and we all drove over to Rockingham County. Tamara Gibson and Dick's cousin Peggy Richardson at the Society of Port Republic Preservationists produced in their files, among other items, a copy of my high school term paper. That long-ago effort had stayed in such general circulation in the neighborhood that Robert K. Krick had found it to quote from in his *Conquering the Valley: Stonewall Jackson at Port Republic* (1996).

Another of Dick's cousins, Graham Lilly, and his wife, Rachel, had just finished restoring Bogota, Graham's ancestral home overlooking the Shenandoah River. We stood on its second-story verandah where, 148 summers before, Lewis family refugees peered helplessly across as the Battle of Port Republic swirled around their homes. We could see one of the homes, Lynnwood, brought back into the family and restored in the 1960s by Dick's brother Thomas B. Dilworth Jr. and his wife, Elizabeth, and their home for more than four decades until their deaths. Beyond, before the river plain was edged by foothills of the distant Blue Ridge, rose the obelisk in the family cemetery, with its graves of seven generations of Lewises.

Not long before, a thousand-page tome had appeared, fifth in the series *Unionists and the Civil War Experience in the Shenandoah Valley*. The series transcribes the lengthy handwritten files of 267 Rockingham County cases considered by the Southern Claims Commission between 1871 and 1880 and presents them in convenient form. This volume includes the Lewis claims I had come upon years before, plus many others filed from that part of the county. It was suddenly a far less daunting task to sift through the broad range of testimonies and synthesize scattered statements, then relate them to the larger historical picture. I am grateful to Norman R. Wenger and David S. Rodes, who compiled the series with editor Dr. Emmett F. Bittinger, for sharing an incident particularly relevant to this book prior to its publication in the sixth—and final—volume.

Appearing on cue to help fill important blanks was Frances Pollard, chief librarian at the Virginia Historical Society in Richmond, where E. Lee Shepard, vice president for collections, was also helpful. Assistant Librarian Katherine Wilkins provided backup support. Brent Tarter at the Library of Virginia provided welcome enthusiasm on the need for studies of Union Loyalists. Dr. Mark E. Peterson, special collections archivist at the James Madison University Libraries, and his interns came up with a little known trove of letters from Charles H. and John F. Lewis. Alexander G. Gilliam Jr., university history officer at the University of Virginia, scoured Board of Visitors minutes from the years Samuel Hance Lewis was a member. Bob Glass at Centre College's library turned up information on Lunsford Lewis's studies there while waiting for the war to end. Lynchburg College Archivist Ariel Myers delved through the late John D. Capron's data on Mount Vernon Furnace.

I am also grateful for the work of those at other institutions, among them the Library of Congress, National Archives and Records Administration, Huntington Library, Duke University, West Virginia University, the Harrisonburg-Rockingham Historical Society, and the San Antonio Public Library. My wife, Mary, has been, as always, supportive and insightful. Our sons, William and Maverick, helped point out lapses in my writing.

Special thanks for reviewing all or portions of the manuscript also go to Brent Tarter, a founding editor of the Library of Virginia's *Dictionary of Virginia Biography* and a cofounder of the annual Virginia Forum; Robert K. Krick, Civil War historian and author of *Conquering the Valley: Stonewall Jackson at Port Republic*; Dr. Jonathan M. Berkey, who teaches the Civil War and Reconstruction at Concord University and has written about the war's effects on civilians in the Shenandoah Valley; Dr. David Libby, who teaches southern history at the University of Texas at San Antonio; Dr. Jonathan E. Helmreich, professor emeritus of history at Allegheny College, my alma mater, and editor of two books of Civil War letters and diaries; and Dr. Richard Lowe, Regents Professor of History at the University of North Texas and author of *Republicans and Reconstruction in Virginia, 1856–70*.

Notes

Abbreviations

RR   *Rockingham Register*
UCWE   *Unionists and the Civil War Experience in the Shenandoah Valley*

Preface

1. Lowe, "John Francis Lewis," *American National Biography*, 13:585.

2. During Reconstruction, Unionists who had opposed the war were lumped by former Confederates with native southern opportunists and scoundrels and vilified under the epithet "scalawag." Observes James Alex Baggett: "Departures from the stereotypical view of scalawags have appeared slowly because of lack of interest about supposedly despicable scalawags. Any more than cursory comments about them are rare in works published before the 1940s" (Baggett, *Scalawags*, 4–5).

1: Samuel Hance Lewis of Lewiston

1. "Answers of L. L. Lewis," *UCWE*, 5:319.

2. Lewis, *Brief Narrative*, 54–55, 57; S. H. Lewis to Lunsford L. Lewis, Dec. 3, 1867, Lewis Family Papers, Virginia Historical Society.

3. Two of Samuel Hance Lewis's responses to Draper, then of Baltimore and later of Madison, Wisconsin, are indexed as Gen. S. H. Lewis to Lyman Draper, Dec. 17, 1844 (SZZ6), and Oct. 29, 1845 (SZZ21) in the Preston and Virginia Papers of the Draper Collection of Manuscripts, State Historical Society of Wisconsin. (The index refers to Samuel Hance Lewis's rank as a brigadier general in the Virginia Militia.) They contain significant details about his grandfather Thomas Lewis and his great-uncle Brig. Gen. Andrew Lewis. His status as a Lewis caused the House of Delegates to name him in 1841 as the Rockingham representative on a committee to collect donations for a state monument planned at the site of the 1774 Battle of Point Pleasant, where his great-uncle Col. Charles Lewis was killed (*Journal of the House of Delegates*, 3:447). A letter cited only as dated Dec. 14, 1855 from Gen. S. H. Lewis "of Augusta County, Virginia" recounts a conversation with former Continental Army Gen. Robert Porterfield of Augusta County, Lewis's onetime commander in the Seventh Brigade of the Virginia Militia, shortly before Porterfield's death. Lewis reports Porterfield recalling Gen. George Washington on his knees at prayer at Valley Forge and, on other occasions, receiving communion. That observation was used in a work by the noted twentieth-century Presbyterian clergyman Peter J. Marshall titled "Was George Washington a Christian?" One version of Marshall's article is online at http-/swordattheready.word-press.com/answering-the-charge-that-george-washington-was-a-deist/.

4. Lewis, *Brief Narrative*, 68.

5. Cowell, "Origins of the John Lewis Family" in Frazier, *Family of John Lewis*, 9–11. Second son Andrew, later a brigadier general in the Continental Army, in 1774

commanded Virginia troops in their victory over the Shawnee at Point Pleasant, where his youngest brother, Col. Charles, a noted frontiersman, was killed. Both served in the House of Burgesses. William ended up in Sweet Springs, now in West Virginia, where he and his family pioneered development of mineral water resort hotels. Perhaps the best among the multitude of accounts of the origins and lives of John Lewis and his sons are the chapters by Mark W. Cowell Jr. in Irvin Frazier's *Family of John Lewis*, 1–76.

6. The quote is from Dumas Malone in *Jefferson and His Time*, 1:23. Such a rise from immigrant status as the Lewises' has traditionally been explained "as proof of the frontier's rich potential for some capable pioneers." Recent scholarship on the Virginia frontier and on Augusta County, however, points to direct involvement of distant property owners among the Tidewater social and political elite, who selected "indeed talented men" on the frontier for key appointments and for access to purchase large tracts of frontier land. Thomas Lewis, for example, Turk McCluskey notes, "received the key post of county surveyor from the president and masters of the College of William and Mary." A carefully picked local elite, in turn, provided reliable oversight of regional development that assured extension of a stable social and political order to Virginia's frontier—"one of the most ingenious frontier policies in British North America, for it ensured that Virginia's periphery was as stable as its core. . . . Virginia's elites spared themselves the frontier upheavals that racked most other colonies over the course of the eighteenth century" (McCluskey, "Rich Land, Poor Prospects," 485–86).

7. Cowell, "Thomas Lewis" in Frazier, *Family of John Lewis*, 32–33.

8. Cowell, "Some Notes on Thomas Lewis's Will," 18; Gilmer, *Sketches of Some of the First Settlers*, 39. At the time of their father's death, the three sons disinherited for having "immoderate" behavior were aged 40, 32 and 30.

9. Fischer and Kelly, *Bound Away*, 178–79; Frazier, *Family of John Lewis*, 83. Frazier recorded only two of the three children as having moved to Saline County, Missouri, but the third was subsequently found to have emigrated there as well.

10. Anne Hance was a cousin of Lewis neighbor John Mackall (Cowell, "Some Notes on Thomas Lewis's Will," 26). Her parental estate, Overton, now the site of a Prince Frederick shopping center, was near the Chesapeake Bay community of Port Republic, offering a suggestion for the origin of the name of the later village established in part by Lewises on the Shenandoah.

11. Meade, *Old Churches, Ministers, and Families*, 2:324–25. The Church of England's Rockingham Parish had been created from Augusta Parish in 1776, though hostility to England caused its two chapels—one near Dayton and the other five miles north of Port Republic on the road to Harrisonburg—to close shortly thereafter. In 1821 Charles Lewis led a fund-raising effort that hired the Rev. Dr. Daniel Stephens, rector of Trinity Episcopal Church in Staunton, to preach in Port Republic once a month for the coming year. Of the twenty-nine contributors, who pledged a total of $115, nearly half were related through the Lewises. The largest individual contributor—of $20, the present-day equivalent of $400—was Charles Lewis's aunt, Margaret Strother Jones, then ninety-five ("Subscriptions for Rev. Mr. Stephens, 1821," author's collection).

12. *Catalog of the Officers and Alumni of Washington and Lee*, 3, 34, 63, 64, 67. Cowell, "Thomas Lewis" in *Family of John Lewis*, 26, 83. Charles's son Thomas is recorded as attending Washington Academy in 1809–10 and Charles Jr. in 1810–11, then Samuel Hance in 1813–14 when it had become Washington College. Chambers & Lewis purchases included such items as six yards of calico, a pair of candlesticks, ten barrels of flour and six scythes. Account records from 1817–18, inherited by the author and analyzed by Mark Cowell, list sundry expenses totaling $2,002, the present-day equivalent of $35,000. Mustoe Chambers, a Staunton native and medical graduate of the University of Pennsylvania, later moved the family to Ohio and on to Iowa, where

he practiced medicine ("Mustoe Chambers," *Tipton (IA) Advertiser*, Sept. 28, 1865).

13. J. Susanne Simmons and Nancy T. Sorrells, "Slave Hire and the Development of Slavery in Augusta County, Virginia" in Koons and Hofstra, *After the Backcountry*, 169–73; Wayland, *History of Rockingham County*, 107; Rockingham County Census, 1810; Koons and Hofstra, *After the Backcountry*, xii–xiii, 3; Bruggeman, "The Shenandoah River Gundalow," 320. In defining a planter class, those who owned five slaves are considered to have been "small planters," those with twenty or more "large planters." The mix of slavery with general farming has been seen as separating the Shenandoah Valley into a "third South," distinct from that of lowland plantations and, in the mountains, the South of subsistence farmers. (Stephen V. Ash, *Middle Tennessee Society Transformed*, 1860–1870: War and Peace in the Upper South, 9–11, in Koons and Hofstra, *After the Backcountry*, xviii.)

14. Jackson and Twohig, eds. *The Diaries of George Washington*, 4:53–56; Bruggeman, "The Shenandoah River Gundalow," 320–22. Also discussed during Washington's visit was Thomas Lewis's surveying knowledge of land Washington owned to the west. Another subject of mutual interest would have been common bonds in Stafford County, where Washington had grown up at Ferry Farm, the home in which the Strother sisters had also lived until their father died prematurely and the home was sold to the Washingtons (Cowell, "Thomas Lewis," Frazier, *Family of John Lewis*, 26). Stuart's mother was Thomas Lewis's daughter Agatha.

15. Bruggeman, "The Shenandoah River Gundalow," 320–25; Frazier, *Family of John Lewis*, 80–81; Greiner, "Navigation and Commerce on the Shenandoah River of Virginia," *The Log of Mystic Seaport* 42:2, 43–45; Ch. Lewis, esq. in a/c with S. H. Lewis, Jan. 1825, author's collection; *The Shenandoah River Atlas*, 35. In February 1817, Charles Lewis offered a work crew superintendent from the previous year, Samuel Coville, the same job for the upcoming season. That suited Coville, though he did express "an objection to work Constant in the water as one of the Hands. I have no wish to avoid work only for reasons which I can State, that is being so long Confined to working in the water it might be a means of bringing on Disease Lasting such as Rieumattic pains &c." (Samuel Coville to Charles Lewis, Feb. 23, 1817, author's collection). Greiner states that the river was open by 1823, but Charles Lewis's accounting lists considerable construction expense into 1824 and shows Nov. 16, 1824 as the date of final completion. Navigation improvements were later made to the North Fork as well. New rail connections at Harpers Ferry extended access to distant markets. The boxlike gundalows that carried freight were generally four feet high, up to ten feet wide and ninety feet long and poled by crews of four to six men. Since the river was not navigable going upstream, at Harpers Ferry the boats could unload their cargoes for reshipment down the wider Potomac and then be sold for their lumber.

16. Shade, *Democratizing the Old Dominion*, 139–41; Gilmer, *Sketches of Some of the First Settlers*, 39; Lewis, *A Brief Narrative*, 53.

17. Lewis, *Brief Narrative*, 53, 54; "Agreement between Samuel H. Lewis and Overton Gibson, Aug. 7, 1826," Lewis Family Papers, Virginia Historical Society; Ann F. McCleary, "Forging a Regional Identity: Development of Rural Vernacular Architecture in the Central Shenandoah Valley, 1790–1850" in Koons and Hofstra, *After the Backcountry*, 92, 103; Susan Lewis Durkee to Lewis Fisher, March 13, 1959; Gilmer, *Sketches of Some of the First Settlers*, 57. A slightly smaller third room at the rear formed an ell, which opened onto a gallery that extended around the back wall of the main house. Beneath was a full cellar. A separate building housed the kitchen. The home faced northward, unlike its present-day successor, which faces southeast. George R. Gilmer remarked upon the front portico's view of the mountain to the north.

18. Lewis, *Family of John Lewis*, 83, 88. Five of Thomas Lewis's five dozen grandchildren married second cousins born in Bath County, where the widow of their great-uncle

Col. Charles Lewis had remained with his children after his death at Point Pleasant in 1774 (Frazier, *Family of John Lewis*, 80–83). Their home and surroundings have been developed as a resort known as Fort Lewis Lodge. Nancy Cameron Lewis was a daughter of Col. Charles Lewis's oldest son, Capt. John Lewis, who married Rachel Miller of Augusta County.

19. Lewis, *Brief Narrative*, 54, 88; "Answers of L. L. Lewis," *UCWE*, 5:323; Wayland, *History of Rockingham County*, 368; Samuel H. Lewis to Lunsford L. Lewis, Jan. 22, 1868, Virginia Historical Society.

20. Wayland, *History of Rockingham County*, 365; J. Susanne Simmons and Nancy T. Sorrells, "Slave Hire and the Development of Slavery in Augusta County, Virginia," in Koons and Hofstra, *After the Backcountry*, 174; "S. H. Lewis, Lewiston, Rockingham, Va. Bible Records," copy in Lewis Family Papers, Virginia Historical Society; "Deposition of Abram James (Colored)," *UCWE*, 5:328. According to one family tradition, Lewiston's slave cemetery was at the foot of the hill northeast of the home and in the 1930s was at least partially covered by U.S. 340, when the old roadway was straightened and the new route was built.

21. Lewis, *Brief Narrative*, 66; Dabney, *Virginia: The New Dominion*, 238. Samuel Hance Lewis seems to have trusted the general common sense of the slave population and doubted fears that John Brown's raid at Harpers Ferry in 1859 would encourage slaves to revolt. He expressed that thought less than a month after the raid in a letter to his late wife's father, John Tayloe Lomax, who agreed. Replied Lomax, who later supported the Confederacy: "Even the ignorance of a slave could not fail to see the madness and the inevitable defeat of [a] scheme so rashly & prematurely carried out, and the folly of his rising to give it any active or express cooperation" (John Tayloe Lomax to S. H. Lewis, Nov. 15, 1859, Lewis Family Papers, Virginia Historical Society).

22. Isaac, *The Transformation of Virginia*, 147–48; E. Allen Coffey, "History of the Diocese of Virginia," www.thediocese.net/Diocesan_Community/History/; Katharine L. Brown, "A Historical Sketch of the Diocese of Southwestern Virginia, www/diosw-va.org:/digital_faith/dfcfiles/31; Waddell, *Annals of Augusta County*, 451; "Subscriptions for Rev. Mr. Stephens, 1821" and "Mrs. Margaret Jones by the hand of Col. S. H. Lewis, May 22, 1822," author's collection.

23. Waddell, *Annals of Augusta County*, 451; *Journal of the Convention of the Protestant Episcopal Church*, 1837, 5–6; 1843–51; 1856, 31–44. He was a delegate to national general conventions in 1838 and 1843 and an alternate in 1847. In 1855 one in the series of Boyden Parish's part-time rectors—the Rev. James C. Wheat, assistant principal of Staunton's church-owned Virginia Female Institute—married Samuel Hance Lewis's daughter Elizabeth. Another clergyman in the family was the Rev. Dr. Charles B. Tippett, who married Samuel Hance Lewis's youngest sister, Margaret, and became a noted Methodist minister in Baltimore.

24. Wayland, *Virginia Valley Records*, 133, 144; Waddell, *Annals of Augusta County*, 257–58; Lunsford Lewis in *A Brief Narrative* (p. 55) suggests that his father may have served in the War of 1812, though his name does not appear in available rosters of Rockingham County volunteers.

25. "Mrs. Margaret Jones by the hand of Col. S. H. Lewis, May 22, 1822," author's collection; "Executive Department to Col. Samuel H. Lewis, Rockingham, Jan. 25, 1837," Lewis Family Papers, Virginia Historical Society; "Brigade Returns, 7th Brigade," 1842–44, Lewis Family Papers, Virginia Historical Society. The Seventh Brigade was made up of men from Rockingham, Augusta, Shenandoah, Page, and Warren counties.

26. Lewis, *Brief Narrative*, 54, 57; "Virginia House of Delegates Election 1824," http://hdl.handle.net/10427/33777; Wayland, *History of Rockingham County*, 441, 443; "New Shenandoah Company," *Staunton Spectator*, Jan 28, 1847, 3. In mid-1847 he represented the company in Front Royal at a convention of delegates from surrounding counties seeking to make the river navigable going upstream. After an engineering

survey the following year, the cost was deemed prohibitive ("Front Royal Convention," *Martinsburg Gazette*, Aug. 12, 1847, 2; Greiner, "Navigation and Commerce on the Shenandoah River of Virginia," *The Log of Mystic Seaport*, 45).

27. As a result of the American Temperance Society's work, "More than 50 distilleries had been stopped, more than 400 merchants had renounced the traffic and more than 1,200 drunkards had ceased to use the drunkard's drink. Persons who a few years before were vagabonds about the street were now sober, respectable men, providing comfortably, by their labor, for their wives and children" ("American Temperance Society," *Permanent Temperance Documents*, 1:28). The extent to which the Lewis family applied the lessons of disinherited relatives is uncertain. Accounts of the Chambers & Lewis cooperative at Lynnwood early in the century include expenses for as many as 36 gallons of "whiskey" and one tab for 90 gallons of brandy, though it is not specified for whom they were purchased. A statement to Charles Lewis in 1824 lists expenses due for materials and labor for construction of a still, no doubt the one that gave the occasional creek past Lynnwood and Lewiston known as Deep Run or Lewis Run its alternate name of Still House Run ("Chambers & Lewis, 1817–18" and "Charles Lewis Esq. to Joseph Points Jr., Sept. 28, 1824," author's collection).

28. "Speech Delivered before a Convention of the Temperance Societies of Rockingham County at Harrisonburg on the 26 of September 1835 by S. H. Lewis," Lewis Family Papers, Virginia Historical Society. The oration's text fills thirty-five small pages, precisely handwritten in nineteen lines per page, and would have taken some forty-five minutes to deliver.

29. Lewis, *Brief Narrative*, 54–55, 58.

2: No to Secession

1. "Slave Inhabitants in District No. 1 in the County of Rockingham, State of Virginia," 23, U.S. Census of 1860. Lewis, *Brief Narrative*, 58, 67–68, 69. Lunsford Lewis added of his father: "The great arguments of Daniel Webster and of John Minor Botts on the subject of the Union he considered unanswerable."

2. "Col. Charles H. Lewis," S. Bassett French Biographical Sketches Collection, *Library of Virginia Online Catalog*, 189; George Derby and James T. White, eds. *National Cyclopaedia of American Biography* 12:128; "Brigade Returns, 7th Brigade," 1842 and 1843, Lewis Family Papers, Virginia Historical Society; J. Lewis Peyton, *History of Augusta County*, 222; Lomax, *Genealogy of the Virginia Family of Lomax*, 24. Charles H. Lewis's wife's name is listed as Ellen in Lewis family sources and in U.S. census records, although it appears as Eleanor in Lomax family genealogies. The marriage made him his father's brother-in-law when, two years later, Ellen's older sister Anna Maria married the widowed Samuel Hance Lewis.

3. "Contributors to the Southern Literary Messenger," *Southern Literary Messenger* 10:1 (January 1844), 3, 4; *Southern Literary Messenger* 8:9 (September 1842), 611; *Staunton Spectator*, Mar. 3, 1842, 1. The first and last of the eight stanzas of "Away from the Haunts of Men":

> Oh! Might I choose a home, I'd fly
>   To yonder pleasant vale,
> Where the crystal stream runs merrily
>   And the wild flowers scent the gale;
>
> With the voice of love to greet me there,
>   Oh! I'd be happy then,—
> Without a wish, without a care,—
>   Away from the haunts of men!

4. Peyton, comp., *Memoir of John Howe Peyton*, 152; Peyton, *History of Augusta County*, 222.

5. *Staunton Spectator*, Jan. 28, 1847, 3; Apr. 1, 1847, 1, 3; Waddell, *Annals of Augusta County*, 257. There is no indication that his wife accompanied Charles H. Lewis to Martinsburg. Spotsylvania County census records list her and their young son and daughter as living with her parents in 1850, a year before her death, after which the children remained with their grandparents. There were high hurdles to divorce in those years, and available records reflect no break in the close relationship between the Lomax and Lewis families. But things were not going well with the son, his grandfather John Tayloe Lomax wrote the other grandfather, Samuel Hance Lewis, when John Tayloe Lomax Lewis was 15. "The indocile waywardness of my dear Tayloe Lewis gives me the deepest concern." Tayloe's disappointing progress in high school was jeopardizing his maternal grandfather's plan to send him to Virginia Military Institute. Judge Lomax was also regularly contributing to the boarding school expenses of his late daughter Anna Lomax Lewis's two eldest children, Charlotte and Lunsford (John Tayloe Lomax to S. H. Lewis, Nov. 15, 1859, Lewis Family Papers, Virginia Historical Society.) Whatever happened after that point, family histories report that Tayloe Lewis died young. His sister, Rebecca, married one John Anderson in 1866, then disappears from family records.

6. *Martinsburg Gazette*, Feb. 25, 1847, 2; "To the Patrons of the Gazette," Mar. 25, 1847, 2.

7. "To the Patrons of the Gazette," *Martinsburg Gazette*, Mar. 25, 1847; Sept. 3, 1847, 2; "Henry Clay," Jan. 6, 1848, 2; "The Triumph of Whig Principles," "Whig Celebration," Dec. 2, 1848, 2. Charles H. Lewis brought with him access to a network of family connections. Bygones were bygones when it came to literary criticism; cousin John Lewis Peyton became the Staunton advertising sales representative for the *Gazette*. In quoting a Richmond speech by George H. Chrisman in support of railroad construction in the Shenandoah Valley, Charles H. Lewis told readers that he could "well conceive of the pleasure with which a speech from him would be listened to by an intelligent assemblage," for "we have known that gentleman from our infancy." When his father was speaking on behalf of the New Shenandoah Company at a Front Royal conference concerning river navigation, the session's chairman was Charles James Faulkner, then Martinsburg's Whig representative in the House of Delegates. Faulkner and Charles H. Lewis discussed state politics, publication of Faulkner's speeches in the *Gazette*, and his impending candidacy for Congress, to which Faulkner was later elected ("Internal Improvements in Virginia," *Martinsburg Gazette*, Sept. 3, 1847, 2; Charles H. Lewis to Charles James Faulkner, Feb. 24, 1849, Faulkner Papers).

8. Maddex, *Virginia Conservatives*, 18; Cappon, *Virginia Newspapers*. Copies of the *Martinsburg Gazette* for 1849–50 are not known to have survived, nor are copies of the *American* during Charles H. Lewis's editorship.

9. Presentation of a Flag," *RR*, Jul. 6, 1860, 3; Charles H. Lewis to John T. Harris, Jan. 5, 1860, John T. Harris Papers. The flag presentation fits the views of those who see the militia as an extension of chivalry, and who cite ceremonies where "defenders of community and fireside" received flags presented by women and young girls. (Kimball, "Militias, Politics and Patriotism," 164–66).

10. Baggett, *Scalawags*, 33.

11. "Opposition Convention," *RR*, Mar. 3, 1860, 2.

12. Our Candidate for President," *RR*, Mar. 3, 1860, 2; "Judge Douglas in Virginia," Sept. 7, 1860, 2; "Presidential Election," Nov. 16, 1860, 2. It was the closest presidential election ever held in Virginia. The several "official" tabulations differ slightly. Basically, Bell beat Breckinridge by less than 400 votes, as the two almost split nearly 150,000 votes. Douglas was a distant third with just over 16,000 votes. Lincoln had upwards

of 1,900. Rockingham County reported 1,354 votes for Douglas, 888 for Bell, 676 for Breckinridge, and none for Lincoln. Bell came in second in Harrisonburg (250 for Bell, 390 for Douglas, 64 for Breckinridge) but at Port Republic was first (96 for Bell, 34 for Douglas, 4 for Breckinridge). In the neighboring former Whig stronghold of Augusta County, Bell received twice as many votes as Douglas—2,553 to 1,094—and ten times as many as Breckinridge. No Augusta votes were recorded for Lincoln.

13. "About the S. Bassett French Biographical Sketches," www.lva.virginia.gov/public/guides/opac/aboutbassettfrench.htm; Samuel Bassett French, "John Francis Lewis," *Library of Virginia Online Catalog*, 191.

14. S. H. Lewis to Hugh W. Sheffey, Jan. 14 1847, Lewis Family File, Society of Port Republic Preservationists. The two-day delay caused the cargo to arrive in Georgetown immediately after a sudden plunge in the price of flour, costing the Lewises as much as $400, about $12,000 in today's dollars. Samuel Hance Lewis wrote to chide son John F.'s cousin-in-law, Hugh Sheffey, then in the House of Delegates, about the need for enforcement of rules against obstacles to river navigation.

15. May, *Port Republic*, 171; John F. Lewis to John T. Harris, Feb. 9, 1861, John T. Harris Papers.

16. "To the People of Rockingham," *RR*, Jan. 25, 1861, 2; Lewis, *Brief Narrative*, 59.

17. "To the People of Rockingham," *RR*, Jan. 25, 1861, 2.

18. "Rockingham Election Official," *RR*, Feb. 8, 1861, 2; "To the People of Rockingham," Jan. 25, 1861, 2.

19. John F. Lewis to John T. Harris, Feb. 9, 1861, John T. Harris Papers. Lewis also wrote Harris: "I defended the little giant [Douglas], and made open war on the Breckinridge men. . . . I wish you to say to Mr. Douglas for me that I take back all that I have ever said against him, and wish he had been (as he deserved to be) elected president. I feel that this humble tribute, from an humble individual like myself, can add nothing to him in any way, but I want to make amends for the injustice unintentionally done him." He added: "My father and Charles . . . cordially return your kind regards. The latter says he concurs in all I have said, and now sincerely regrets not having voted for you."

20. "Rockingham Election Official," *RR*, Feb. 8, 1861, 2; "To the People of Rockingham," Jan. 25, 1861, 2.

21. "Handsomely Done," *RR*, Jun. 9, 1860, 2; *Baltimore American*, quoted in "Election of a Whig in Rockingham," Mar. 1, 1861, 2.

22. "Election of a Whig in Rockingham," *RR*, Mar. 1, 1861, 2. *Register* comments were even more circuitous following the withdrawal of a Unionist candidate it had long opposed—George H. Chrisman, 62, one of Samuel Hance Lewis's closest friends: "The withdrawal of this gentleman's name as a candidate for the Convention, just on the eve of the election, excited the surprise of almost everybody. Justice to Mr. Chrisman, who has been our long-time political opponent, requires us to say that in our judgment his election was 'a fixed fact' had he remained upon the track. Some of his warmest friends, however, thought there was danger of his election, and advised his withdrawal. He was regarded by the great mass of the Union men of the county as the very embodiment of their sentiments; hence, their votes must, under that impression, have been cast for him almost unanimously. Besides, his age, intelligence and unsullied integrity made all the people willing to ignore and forget, for the time, former differences of opinion which have separated Mr. Chrisman from the sympathies of the great body of the people of Rockingham." ("Geo. H. Chrisman Esq.," *RR*, Feb. 8, 1861, 2). Chrisman's wife, Martha, happened to be a second cousin of Abraham Lincoln, whose father was born in Rockingham County. ("Chrisman/Hite Family," retrieved Aug. 25, 2011, www.georgechrismanhouse.com/8.html). In another local Lincoln connection, the president's first cousin, also named Abraham Lincoln, had been a militia colonel commanding the 116th Regiment under Brig. Gen. Samuel Hance Lewis in the 1840s

("Brigade Returns, 7th Brigade," 1842–44, Lewis Family Papers, Virginia Historical Society).

23. John F. Lewis to John T. Harris, Feb. 9, 1861, John T. Harris Papers.

24. Reese, ed., *Proceedings*, 1:795.

25. Freehling and Simpson, eds., *Showdown in Virginia*, x–xi. The seven states of the Lower South were South Carolina, Mississippi, Florida, Alabama, Georgia, Louisiana, and Texas. The editors note that of the tier of border states in the Upper South—Delaware, Maryland, Kentucky, and Missouri—none seceded. Of the Middle South states forming the lower tier of the Upper South—Virginia, North Carolina, Tennessee, and Arkansas—secession occurred only after the war started.

26. *Report of the Joint Committee*, 2:117; "Correspondence of the Register," *RR*, Mar. 1, 1861, 1; John F. Lewis to John T. Harris, Feb. 19, 1861 and Mar. 3, 1861, John T. Harris Papers. If John F. Lewis needed any reminder about his family's role in putting the nation together, he had only to look to the square outside the capitol building, where the first secession convention sessions were held. There, unveiled three years earlier, stood—and stands—a monumental twenty-foot equestrian statue of George Washington on a forty-foot granite pedestal, surrounded by twelve-foot bronze statues of six Virginian Revolutionary War era patriots—Patrick Henry, Thomas Jefferson, John Marshall, George Mason, Thomas Nelson, and Andrew Lewis, John F. Lewis's great-great uncle.

27. "Correspondence of the Register," *RR*, Mar. 1, 1861, 1, and Mar. 8, 1861, 2; John F. Lewis to Serena S. Lewis, Feb. 28, 1861, author's collection.

28. Crofts, *Reluctant Confederates*, 308.

29. John F. Lewis to John T. Harris, Mar. 3, 1861, Mar. 8, 1861, and Mar. 15, 1861, John T. Harris Papers.

30. Freehling and Simpson, eds., *Showdown in Virginia*, x, xvi, 75, 172; "Testimony of John F. Lewis," *Report of the Joint Committee*, 2:70, 71; John F. Lewis to John T. Harris, Feb. 19, 1861, Mar. 8, 1861, and Mar. 15, 1861, John T. Harris Papers. Lewis had taken Baldwin to visit Botts, who concluded that Baldwin had not properly considered or conveyed Lincoln's proposal to withdraw troops from Fort Sumter if the Virginia convention rejected secession.

31. Crofts, *Reluctant Confederates*, 309–12; Freehling and Simpson, eds., *Showdown in Virginia*, xiv, xvi–xvii.

32. Freehling and Simpson, eds., *Showdown in Virginia*, x, xvi, 75, 172.

33. Freehling and Simpson, eds., *Showdown in Virginia*, xvii; "Answers of William D. Maiden," *UCWE*, 5:59, "Deposition of Charles Douglas Gray," 5:726. Virginia voting in presidential elections was by ballot, but voters first had to ask for a ticket bearing the name of their candidate before casting the slip as a vote.

34. "Answers of William D. Maiden, *UCWE*, 5:59, "Answers of Andrew J. Baugher," 5:173; "Deposition of D. S. Lewis," 5:261, "Answers of Elias Hudlow," 5:276; "Deposition of Charles Douglas Gray," 5:726–27; Lewis, *Brief Narrative*, 60.

35. "Make War for Rockingham!," *RR*, May 24, 1861, 2.

36. "Introduction," *UCWE*, 5:12; "Make War for Rockingham!," *RR*, May 24, 1861, 2; "Deposition of Louisa Shifflet," *UCWE*, 5:298, "Testimony of Samuel H. Lewis Jr.," 5:347; "Testimony of Amos Scott," 5:370.

37. Julienne and Tarter, "The Virginia Ordinance," 154–81; Lowe, "John Francis Lewis" in *American National Biography*, 13:584.

3: Cannon Fire Interrupts Breakfast

1. "Answers of L. L. Lewis," *UCWE*, 5:320. According to 122 transaction records that survive from the camp near Winchester, in August 1861 regimental quartermaster

Capt. Samuel H. Lewis Jr. issued nearly 32 cords of firewood, approximately 3 tons of hay, more than 21 bushels of oats, more than 14 bushels of corn, 2 axes, 6 pounds of nails, 5 camp kettles, 2 tin buckets, 2 mess pans, 1 pair of scales, 7 coffee mills, 4 skillets with lids, 360 sheets of writing paper, and 1 bottle of ink (Lewis Family Papers, author's collection).

2. "Testimony of Charles H. Lewis," *Report of the Joint Committee*, 2:146.

3. "Return of the Militia," *RR*, Sept. 18, 1861, 2. The militia force totaled 781. The rest were reported out sick or on leave.

4. *Report of the Joint Committee*, 2:70.

5. "Testimony of L. L. Lewis," *UCWE*, 5:344, "Testimony of John F. Lewis," 5:345–46. Riverside is one of the oldest homes in the area. Its original eighteenth-century section is of logs covered with clapboards.

6. "Deposition of Charles Lewis Jr.," *UCWE*, 5:64, "Answers of L. L. Lewis," 5:320; "Rockingham Rifles," *RR*, Aug. 16, 1861, 2.

7. J. M. Berkey, (March 15, 2010). "Rockingham Rebellion," E*ncyclopedia Virginia*: http://www.EncyclopediaVirginia.org/Rockingham_Rebellion, retrieved January 6, 2012. Berkey observes: "The Rockingham Rebellion marked an important shift away from leniency and toward severe government action against offending soldiers and civilians, a shift made possible by the establishment of a more firm executive authority in Richmond by 1862. Confederate president Jefferson Davis also enjoyed the political will to enforce these actions, as Confederate citizens began to grasp the nature of the wartime crisis." Ironically, the Rockingham Rebellion was put down by a Confederate brigadier general from Rockingham County, John R. Jones of Harrisonburg.

8. Hotchkiss, *Make Me a Map*," 33–35.

9. Hotchkiss, *Make Me a Map*," 35; "Answers of L. L. Lewis," *UCWE*, 5:321–22; Krick, *Conquering the Valley*, 470.

10. Hotchkiss, *Make Me a Map*," 35–36.

11. "Deposition of John F. Lewis," *UCWE*," 5:325; Krick, *Conquering the Valley*, 470; "Testimony of L. L. Lewis," *UCWE* 5:345. John F. Lewis's complaint was made sixteen years later to Southern Claims commissioners hearing a claim for property seized by the Union Army at Lewiston without promised compensation. Had he or other family members admitted to receiving compensation for property taken by the Confederate Army, it would have called their Union loyalty into question and jeopardized compensation for their U.S. claims. "They seem determined not to pay any one that they can get an excuse for refusing," he once wrote of commissioners in frustration over another's claim, an observation echoed by some historians (John F. Lewis to William S. Downs, May 15, 1874 in May, Port Republic, 258). In testimony in 1871 on behalf of his claim for compensation for loss of his horses and fence rails, Samuel H. Lewis Jr. stated that he "never furnished any supplies" to the Confederate government, and that "I had corn taken by the Confederate government, received no pay for it." It seems, indeed, that it is his father's scratched signature on a September 1864 receipt for fifteen bushels of corn. That document bears the unusual notation "Union Man," hinting that the seller was not totally happy with the transaction and made some point to the Confederate quartermaster. It is certainly his father's signature on a receipt four days earlier for twelve bushels of corn and 250 pounds of fodder, and on a February 1864 receipt for 3,350 pounds of baled straw sold to the Confederate Army for $60.30 ("Testimony of Samuel H. Lewis," *UCWE*, 5:341; "Archive Office," 5:348–49; "John F. Lewis," "Samuel H. Lewis," Confederate Papers, M346). Several years after Samuel H. Lewis Jr.'s claim was denied for issues other than validity of the loss, clerks in the Archive Office of the U.S. War Department placed into his file three notations of transactions found in Confederate records, though one—$720 for 96 barrels of flour on Sept. 4, 1862—apparently did not involve him. That bears the notation "We have not

the signature & the paper does not show locality of the transaction," though it was assigned anyway to this Samuel H. Lewis. The case for mistaken identity is strengthened by the number of barrels, most likely in the stock of a mill. It was his brother John F., however, who was in charge of the Lynnwood mill and who would have been compensated instead, as he had been five months earlier. Nor did that receipt apparently have sufficient merit to pass others' screening and make it into the Samuel H. Lewis M346 file in the National Archives ("Testimony of Samuel H. Lewis," UCWE, 5:341; "Samuel H. Lewis," Confederate Papers, M346).

12. Hotchkiss, Make Me a Map," 35–36; Krick, Conquering the Valley, 4–5.

13. Krick, Conquering the Valley, 6–7. Fremont had also been, in 1856, the Republican Party's first candidate for president.

14. "From Fremont's Army," New York Times, Jun. 18, 1862, 1.

15. Krick, Conquering the Valley, 41–42; Lewis, Brief Narrative, 55; "Testimony of Amos Scott," UCWE, 5:373.

16. Krick, Conquering the Valley, 124, 126–27. The coaling also furnished charcoal for Lewiston's domestic use (Susan Lewis Durkee to Lewis Fisher, Jan. 8, 1959).

17. Anne Mays Miller to Lewis Fisher, Apr. 7, 1959; "The Family of William Claiborne Walton and Lucinda Muse," www.trakwest.com/zwal36.htm, retrieved Oct. 22, 2010; Frazier, Family of John Lewis, 314; "Deposition of Evaline A. Baugher," UCWE, V:191. Charles Lewis's eldest son Thomas, who inherited the home, had died in 1840, leaving Lynnwood with his widow, Delia Fletcher Lewis, 26, and their only child, six-month-old Anne. In October 1861, Anne's husband, Robert Hall Walton, 28, a Presbyterian minister in nearby Broadway, left on assignment as chaplain to a Confederate unit in Georgia. To manage the estate, Delia's father, Richard P. Fletcher, moved to Lynnwood with his wife and other children. Census records show that by 1860 Delia and her father had moved back to Harrisonburg, putting Delia's brother, Richard Jr., in charge.

18. Krick, Conquering the Valley, 126, 130. The name of the home, from that of the capital of Colombia, is pronounced buh-GOTE-ah, and was bestowed during the enthusiasm in the United States for the recent independence movements in South America. Bogota and its outbuildings were restored by a great-great-grandson of Jacob Strayer, Graham C. Lilly, and his wife, Rachel, and in 2008 were added to the National Register of Historic Places.

19. "Deposition of A. L. Wagner," UCWE, 5:343–44, "Testimony of L. L. Lewis, 5:345.

20. "Deposition of Abram James (Colored)," UCWE, 5:328–30, "The Petition of Winfield Scott Baugher," 5:187; "Deposition of Emanuel Doubt (Colored)," 5:195.

21. Partial transcript of Lucy Muse Walton Fletcher's 1862 diary, author's collection; Lillian McFarland to Lewis Fisher, Mar. 14, 1959.

22. This incident is one of those reported to diarist Lucy Muse Walton Fletcher in Richmond from her Fletcher relatives at Lynnwood. The accounts were provided in 1959 by Anne Mays Miller and a Florida cousin, Lillian McFarland, who had turned up her great-grandmother's diaries in a trunk two years before. Although Lucy Fletcher's oft-quoted 1864–65 diary is now at Duke University, present whereabouts of the one from 1862 with these reports is unknown.

23. Partial transcript of Lucy Muse Walton Fletcher's 1862 diary, author's collection; Frazier, Family of John Lewis, 96; Miller to Fisher, Jul. 30, 1959; Strayer diary.

24. Krick, Conquering the Valley, 292, 304, 306; Lewis, Brief Narrative, 61; Durkee to Fisher, Mar. 4, 1959; Fletcher 1862 diary transcript.

25. Strayer diary; Krick, Conquering the Valley, 288–89. In her diary, Clara Strayer says the first artillery fire came at 6 a.m. However, in Conquering the Valley (pp. 306, 544) Robert Krick reports that "at least fourteen sources offer times for the opening Union round," ranging from 5 to 9 a.m. Krick's analysis puts the actual time at about 7:30.

26. Strayer diary; Fletcher 1862 diary transcript; Frazier, *Family of John Lewis*, 316; Krick, *Conquering the Valley*, 302.

27. Krick, *Conquering the Valley*, 308, 311–12, 323, 457; Strayer diary.

28. Krick, *Conquering the Valley*, 457.

29. Krick, *Conquering the Valley*, 465–66, 469–71; Strayer diary.

30. Krick, *Conquering the Valley*, 470, 474–75, 485; Hotchkiss, *Make Me a Map*, 55–56.

31. Anna Louisa Sheffey to Oliver P. Baldwin, Jun. 11, 1862, Baldwin Family Papers; Krick, *Conquering the Valley*, 470, 474.

32. "Deposition of John F. Lewis," George H. Chrisman Claim #9729 in Southern Claims Commission files, Military Reference Branch, National Archives. The account was uncovered and kindly provided by editors Norman Wenger and David Rodes in advance of the claim's inclusion in Volume 6 of *Unionists and the Civil War Experience in the Shenandoah Valley*, forthcoming in 2013.

33. Hotchkiss, *Make Me a Map*, 56; Krick, *Conquering the Valley*, 495.

34. Fletcher 1862 diary transcript.

35. Fletcher 1862 diary transcript. Bogota suffered from marauding soldiers when artillery was placed nearby after the Battle of Port Republic. They "stripped it of all edibles" and went on to the smokehouse and dairy, until Clara Strayer appealed to a captain on Fremont's staff and the soldiers were sent off. The ailing Jacob Strayer, his clothing stolen, was left "with scarcely a change of linen" (Strayer diary; *RR*, Jun. 27, 1862, 1).

36. Colt, *Defending the Valley*, 213; "Answers of L. L. Lewis," *UCWE*, 5:321, 345, "Deposition of Abram James (Colored)," 5:329; Krick, *Conquering the Valley*, 483.

37. Krick, *Conquering the Valley*, 482.

38. *RR*, Jun. 27, 1862, 1; "Testimony of Amos Scott," *UCWE*, 5:372.

39. Berkey, "The Valley's Civilians" in Gallagher, ed., *Shenandoah Valley Campaign of 1862*, 91; *RR*, Jul. 7, 1862, 2.

40. Miller to Fisher, Jul. 30, 1959; Frazier, *Family of John Lewis*, 96.

41. Colt, *Defending the Valley*, 212.

42. Colt, *Defending the Valley*, 213.

4: John F. Lewis's Private War

1. Baggett, *Scalawags*, 66, 74, 77, 88; Bynum, *Shadow of the Civil War*, 15–16; Dyer, *Secret Yankees*, 28, 52. Botts was freed after he agreed to leave the city—he found a new home in Culpeper County—though others were transferred to a military prison in North Carolina, where they stayed until being exchanged that fall with Union hostages.

2. "Testimony of William J. Points," *UCWE*, 5:93, "Deposition of Charles Lewis," 5:64, "Deposition of Algernon S. Gray,"5:64.

3. Bittinger, ed., *UCWE*, 5:ix–x, 5, 10, 12, "Answers of L. L. Lewis," 5:320.

4. Wayland, *History of Rockingham County*, 353.

5. "Deposition of John F. Lewis," *UCWE*, 5:325.

6. "Answers of L. L. Lewis," *UCWE*, 5:320, 344, "Testimony of William D. Maiden," V:67. Maiden also said in his testimony, given in 1900: "My grandfather fought for the Union in the Revolutionary War, my father fought for it in the War of 1812 and I was unwilling to have it destroyed, and opposed it all I could," although "I have been persecuted, ostracized and proscribed for it ever since."

7. "Testimony of William D. Maiden,"*UCWE*, 5:91.

8. "Testimony of William D. Maiden,"*UCWE*, 5:91. Maiden worked with Abraham L. Wagner, exempt from Confederate military service as the miller. N. J. Wagner, six years older than Abraham, also did "milling, some," but his basic assignment was at

the furnace (Deposition of N. J. Wagner, *UCWE*, 5:77).

9. May, *Port Republic*, 254–55; Heatwole, *The Burning*, 75; Krick, *Conquering the Valley*, 128; George H. Walker, "Defendants' Supplemental Brief," *UCWE*, 5:95.

10. Capron, "Virginia Iron Furnaces," 14; "Deposition of John Harshbarger," *UCWE*, 5:113.

11. May, *Life Under Four Flags*, 212–13; Whisonant, "Geology and History of the Civil War Iron Industry," 1; Lesley, *Iron Manufacturer's Guide*, 180; May, *My Augusta*, 412–13; Swank, *History of the Manufacture of Iron*, 3:268, 508. Henry Miller, who early on bought out a partner, produced wrought iron farm utensils, stoves and cooking utensils, plus cannonballs for colonial troops in the American Revolution In his *Notes on the State of Virginia*, Thomas Jefferson listed Miller's iron works as one of two in the Shenandoah Valley in 1781, and one of five in Virginia. In 1784 Henry Miller built near his operation a landmark two-story stone home, one of the earliest large houses in the region, which survives, restored. The relationship of John Miller to the other Millers, however, is unclear. Henry "Iron Man" Miller had no son by that name, and Samuel Miller's son John is reported as moving to Missouri with his other brothers early on and shows in census records as having stayed there. That he could have been a nephew of Samuel Miller is suggested by the common name and occupation and by John's future relationship with a documented grandson of Henry Miller, William G. Miller.

12. May, *Port Republic*, 222; Wayland, "Brown's Gap Turnpike"; Hotchkiss, "The Shenandoah Valley Railroad," 37. The site may have been in use for iron production two decades before construction of the furnace. Archeologists cite the possibility of construction there in the 1820s of a bloomery, a primitive type of iron furnace built around a pit or chimney (Ellis, "Mount Vernon Furnace," 1).

13. May, *Life Under Four Flags*, 249; May, *My Augusta*, 415; Lesley, *Iron Manufacturer's Guide*, 69, 180. The furnace's beginning is put at 1830 in Lambert, *Undying Past* (p. 80) based on an earlier source, which apparently conflated Mount Vernon Forge, which Miller took over in 1830, with Mount Vernon Furnace, begun the next decade and first named Margaret Jane Furnace.

14. Capron, "Virginia Iron Furnaces," 13.

15. Capron, "Virginia Iron Furnaces," 13; Lesley, *Iron Manufacturer's Guide*, 180; Grattan, *Reports of Cases Decided*, 32:103.

16. This appears to be Joseph Smith of nearby Folly Mills, a large landholder with ties to some families involved in the furnace's restructuring and who made loans to numerous enterprises in the area ("A Guide to the Folly Farm Papers," University of Virginia Alderman Library, ead.lib.virginia.edu/vivaead/published/uva-sc/viu00097.document).

17. Grattan, *Reports of Cases Decided*, 32:103–05; Peyton, *History of Augusta County*, 314–15; Lewis, *Brief Narrative*, 55.

18. Miller's wife also had an ownership interest, having released her contingent interest in her husband's property in exchange for a one-third interest in the trust, preserving one asset for the family of seven. Her "contingent right of dower" was successfully challenged in court in 1879 by a lien holder ignored in the original payments. The widowed Mary Miller and her children were required to pay that creditor their share of his debt (Grattan, *Reports of Cases Decided*, 32:105).

19. "Free Inhabitants of District No. 1 in the County of Rockingham, State of Virginia," U.S. Census for 1860, 305–30. That tally of workers does not include unidentified slaves who may have also been working at the furnace at that time. In 1850 John Miller, by then among Rockingham County's largest slaveholders, owned fifty-four male slaves between the ages of 25 and 50, plus another eight who were younger or female ("Slave Inhabitants of the 56½ District in the County of Rockingham, State of Virginia," U.S. Census for 1850, 9–10). A hint that the furnace may have shut down for

an extended period comes from a passing remark by Amos Scott, who referred to his son being employed there by John F. Lewis "as soon as the Iron Works were started" ("Deposition of Amos Scott," *UCWE*, 5:358).

20. Capron, "Virginia Iron Furnaces," 13.

21. "To the Voters of the Sixth Congressional District," *RR*, Oct. 6, 1865, 1. Indeed, one motivation for the move was "to benefit my condition pecuniarily," he once stated. (The last word appears as "pecuniary" in "Deposition of John F. Lewis," *UCWE*, 5:324, though it is "pecuniarily" in the original transcript of the deposition.)

22. "Testimony of John F. Lewis," *UCWE*, 5:346; *Report of the Joint Committee*, 2:148; "Free Inhabitants in New Market in the County of Shenandoah, State of Virginia," U.S. Census for 1860, 106; Peyton, *History of Augusta County*, 314; "Deposition of John F. Lewis," *UCWE*, 5:324; May, *My Augusta*, 415. Since the transfer to Benjamin Crawford and Joseph Smith in 1860, Smith had been replaced as an owner by Staunton physician Briscoe Baldwin Donaghe and by Donaghe's brother-in-law James A. Cochran of Loch Willow, Augusta County. Cochran was a second cousin of William G. Miller and had served in the militia in the 1840s as 7th Brigade quartermaster on the staff of Brig. Gen. Samuel Hance Lewis ("Brigade Returns, 7th Brigade," 1842–44, Lewis Family Papers, Virginia Historical Society). A fourth new owner along with John F. Lewis, Crawford and Manasseh Blackburn was Horatio B. Meason, otherwise unidentified. C. E. May reports in *My Augusta* (p. 415) that the conveyance to Benjamin Crawford and Joseph Smith occurred on September 9, 1861, although a definitive court case states that happened nine months earlier (Grattan, *Reports of Cases Decided*, 32:105). May also reports the conveyance to John F. Lewis et.al. as occurring in 1863, although sworn testimony by Blackburn (*Report of the Joint Committee*, 2:148) states that he was already there in 1862, and immediately after the battle that June Stonewall Jackson's headquarters are uniformly recorded as in John F. Lewis's home at the furnace. The discrepancies may reflect May's reporting of delayed dates on which the conveyances were finally recorded in county records.

23. Lesley, *Iron Manufacturer's Guide*, 69, 591; Whisonant, "Geology and History of the Civil War Iron Industry," 31; Reeder and Reeder, *Shenandoah Secrets*, 159–60; Lambert, *Undying Past*, 81.

24. May, *My Augusta*, 415; Capron, "Virginia Iron Furnaces," 13; Whisonant, "Geology and History of the Civil War Iron Industry," 31; Forest Service, "The Historic Iron and Charcoaling Industries."

25. Capron, "Virginia Iron Furnaces," 14; "Deposition of John F. Lewis," *UCWE*, 5:325; "Lewis and Crawford," Confederate Papers, M346; Lesley, *Iron Manufacturer's Guide*, 69. Seven vouchers made it into Confederate civilian business files now available, dated from April 6 to October 17, 1863. From the sequence it appears that iron was taken to the Staunton Ordnance Depot every two weeks. Whether the iron had been claimed forcibly or not, Lewis and Crawford received in the range of $600 a ton.

26. Capron, "Virginia Iron Furnaces," 14; "Testimony of Manasseh Blackburn," *Report of the Joint Committee*, 2:148.

27. "Testimony of Manasseh Blackburn," *Report of the Joint Committee*, 2:148. No Mount Vernon vouchers survive in Confederate business papers from Oct. 17, 1863 to Jan. 20, 1864, which could reflect a normal period of several months each year when iron furnaces shut down for maintenance. The last two vouchers extant, dated Jan. 20 and Mar. 10, 1864, differ in form from the previous year's, apparently due to the change of contracts. Those from 1864 state that the orders for iron—also taken to the Staunton Ordnance Depot—were issued by the commander of the "Richmond Arsenals," Col. W. L. Brown, for the manufacture of horseshoes and nails. Payment for the two vouchers went up from the previous $600 a ton to $800, despite John F. Lewis's written assertion that the new contract "*did not pay*" (italics his), perhaps a reference

to transactions whose records did not survive ("Lewis and Crawford," Confederate Papers, M346; "To the Voters of the Sixth Congressional District," *RR*, Oct. 6, 1865, 1).

28. "To the Voters of the Sixth Congressional District," *RR*, Oct. 6, 1865, 1.

29. "Deposition of Levi Pirkey," *UCWE*, 5:61, "Deposition of Amos Scott," 5:358–59; "Deposition of Michael A. Scott," 5:362; "Testimony of Amos Scott," 5:372.

30. "Deposition of Matilda Crawford," *UCWE*, 5:208, "Deposition of Lawrence Crawford," V:215, 225. An implication that John F. Lewis was duplicitous in his Union loyalism by willingly accepting aid from Confederate soldiers "when production demands warranted extra laborers" is made in Heatwole, *The Burning*, 75. Its authority, however, is one vague and ill-described citation. Such a conclusion may have originated from active duty Confederate soldiers who were covert Union Loyalists having been transferred to work at Mount Vernon Furnace. There was certainly duplicity in the operation, but that would have been, instead, John F. Lewis's representation that he needed workers when there was in reality no shortage, the need being, rather, to shelter Union Loyalists.

31. "Testimony of William D. Maiden," *UCWE*, 5: 91, 111, "Deposition of Andrew J. Baugher," 5:172.

32. "Deposition of Lawrence Crawford," *UCWE*, 5:215.

5. North with Sheridan

1. "Testimony of John F. Lewis," *Report of the Joint Committee*, 2:72.

2. Strayer," Diary.

3. Gallagher, ed., *Shenandoah Valley Campaign of 1864*, ix; Charles H. Lewis to John T. Harris, Jan. 19, 1864, John T. Harris Papers. Charles H. Lewis's continuing presence near Lewiston eliminates him as the Charles H. Lewis listed as an engrossing clerk at the Restored Government of Virginia's Second General Assembly, held in Alexandria at the same time. He is also sometimes confused with the contemporary Charles H. Lewis who lived in Jefferson County.

4. Gallagher, ed., *Shenandoah Valley Campaign of 1864*, ix–xiii, 7, 9, 24; William G. Thomas, "Nothing Ought to Astonish Us: Confederate Civilians in the 1864 Shenandoah Valley Campaign", in Gallagher, ed., *Shenandoah Valley Campaign of 1864*, 226–27, 237.

5. "Testimony of L. L. Lewis," *UCWE*, 5:345. A candidate for the identity of the staff officer who knew Samuel Hance Lewis is a distant cousin of Lewis's, Brig. Gen. David Hunter Strother. Born in the lower Shenandoah Valley and also a strong Unionist, Strother had gone so far as to join the Union Army. He became chief of staff to a closer cousin, Maj. Gen. David Hunter. Strother's diaries, published as *A Virginia Yankee in the Civil War*, record his presence with Hunter in the Port Republic area in June 1864. Strother was also the noted writer and illustrator who used the pen name Porte Crayon.

6. William G. Thomas, "Nothing Ought to Astonish Us" in Gallagher, ed., *Shenandoah Valley Campaign of 1864*, 240–41; Heatwole, *The Burning*, 130; *Encyclopedia Virginia*, Brendan Wolfe, ed., 2 Feb. 2012, Virginia Foundation for the Humanities, 15 Sep. 2010, www.EncyclopediaVirginia.org/Shenandoah_Valley_During_the_Civil_War.

7. "Deposition of Isaac Bowman," *UCWE*, 5:565–66. Bowman was paid $515 of his claim for $1,406. Southern Claims commissioners decided that amount covered those items "taken and consumed on the farm or in the vicinity by Sheridan's Command" but disallowed the livestock driven off as not having been "army supplies," and therefore ineligible for a claim ("Remarks," *UCWE*, 5:575).

8. Wayland, *Virginia Valley Records*, 195; Heatwole, *The Burning*, 74; Capron, "Virginia's Iron Furnaces," 17. Of the 71 flour mills in Rockingham County, 39 others

were also spared. A grandson of John F. Lewis said that Sheridan's troops started to burn the mill but the fire was put out because it would have endangered nearby homes (M. Botts Lewis to Lewis Fisher, Aug. 6, 1957). A mill near Dayton that was full of grain was not burned for the same reason (Wayland, *Virginia Valley Records*, 195). John F. Lewis had another answer, at a war claims hearing thirteen years later. A standard interrogatory asked how the speaker's Union loyalty would have been demonstrated through special protections granted him. John F. Lewis responded by stating that when Sheridan was burning mills in the Valley, "he refused to burn mine on account of my loyalty" ("Deposition of John F. Lewis," *UCWE*, 5:325). Yet another explanation—the least likely—comes indirectly from onetime mill worker N. J. Wagner, whom a relative said told her that "the only reason" Sheridan did not burn the mill was because of "the need for grain to be ground for the Yanks" (Downs, *Mills of Rockingham County*, 1:68).

9. Cheney, *History of the Ninth Regiment*, 225; Hotchkiss, *Make Me a Map*, 232–33; Confederate Papers, M346. Receipts were dated September 24 and 26, and totaled $111.75.

10. *War of the Rebellion*, 43(1):477; Cheney, *History of the Ninth Regiment*, 225–26.

11. "Deposition of George Miller," *UCWE*, 5:107, "Deposition of William T. Coleman," 5:194.

12. "Deposition of N. J. Wagner," *UCWE*, 5:78, "Deposition of William D. Maiden," 5:80–81;

13. "Deposition of Henry Crawford," *UCWE*, 5:212, "Deposition of Lawrence Crawford," 5:225.

14. "Answers of L. L. Lewis," *UCWE*, 5:318–20; Lomax, *Genealogy of the Virginia Family of Lomax*, 24, 39, 42. In March 1865 Robert E. Lee named General Lomax to succeed Jubal Early as commander of the valley district.

15. Murphy, *10th Virginia Infantry*, 160; "Answers of L. L. Lewis," *UCWE*, 5:320. The latter reference, the only known account of William M. Lewis's departure from the Army, states that he left when his term of enlistment expired—although whether or not he actually deserted, at his age he would still have been required to reenlist.

16. "Answers of L. L. Lewis," *UCWE*, 5:318–19, "Deposition of William S. Downs," 5:246; Beale, ed., *Diary of Edward Bates*, 417.

17. Heatwole, *The Burning*, 130–31, quoting from Peter S. Hartman, *Reminiscences of the Civil War* (Lancaster, PA: Eastern Mennonite Associated Libraries and Archives, 1964); Strayer, Diary.

18. Heatwole, *The Burning*, 130–31, quoting from Peter S. Hartman, *Reminiscences of the Civil War*.

19. "Deposition of Lawrence Crawford," *UCWE* 5:214, "Remarks," 5:575; "Deposition of D. S. Lewis," 5:261; "Deposition of William S. Downs," 5:246. According to George May, Sheffey Lewis was dispatched on horseback by his father, John F. Lewis, to defend Downs before Union officers. (May, *Port Republic, 257.*)

20. Beale, ed., *Diary of Edward Bates*, 418; "Answers of L. L. Lewis," *UCWE*, 5:320; "Speech of Robert A. Gray," 5:1059.

21. Lomax, *Genealogy of the Virginia Family of Lomax*, 38–39; Lunsford L. Lewis to Charles H. Lewis, Mar. 30, 1865 in Lunsford Lomax Lewis Papers. Living 100 miles north of Keokuk—in Tipton—were another uncle and aunt, Dr. Mustoe and Mary Anne Lewis Chambers, who came from Virginia by way of Ohio. Their son Dr. Charles Lewis Chambers, born near Lynnwood and Lunsford's first cousin, was serving as a surgeon with the 35th Iowa Infantry.

22. Bob E. Glass, Centre College, to Lewis F. Fisher, Jul. 23 and Jul. 29, 2010; Lunsford L. Lewis to Charles H. Lewis, Mar. 30, 1865 in Lunsford Lomax Lewis Papers, Huntington Library. In the library's description of the letter from Lunsford Lewis, the brother in the salutation "My Dear Brother" is misidentified as being John F. Lewis.

23. Beale, ed., *Diary of Edward Bates*, 426–27; Goode, *Virginia Cousins*, 368. A third Gray brother, Algernon, had fled Harrisonburg to live in Baltimore for the rest of the war (Wayland, *History of Rockingham County*, 353).

24. Before the war Governor Pierpont had been a lawyer and pioneer coal operator in western Virginia. An oft-cited example of his early determination to succeed is his having walked 180 miles from his home into western Pennsylvania to attend Allegheny College.

25. Lunsford L. Lewis to Charles H. Lewis, Mar. 30, 1865 in Lunsford Lomax Lewis Papers; "Testimony of Charles H. Lewis," *Report of the Joint Committee*, 2:144; Secretary of the Commonwealth Records, Series 1, General Correspondence 1865, Library of Virginia.

26. "Speech of Robert A. Gray," *UCWE*, 5:1059, 1061.

6. Moderates in the Postwar Tumult

1. "Deposition of Robert A. Gray," UCWE, 5:721.

2. Testimony of Charles Douglas Gray," *Report of the Joint Committee*, 2:68.

3. Frazier, *Family of John Lewis*, 310; Anne Mays Miller to Lewis Fisher, Feb. 16, 1959. The "additional compensation" could have come from John F. Lewis's proceeds from the sale of Mount Vernon Furnace after the war, when "moneys from Virginia" helped pay for the Waltons' new house in Kingston, Georgia. Whatever the compensation, it was sufficient to keep the families on good terms for the next several generations, though having to give up Lynnwood "was the tragedy of her life," wrote her granddaughter Anne Miller. Robert Walton served a Presbyterian church in Kingston until his death in 1876, at the age of 43. His wife died at 80, in 1920, and was remembered as "a tiny woman who played the piano and wore dainty little lace trimmed aprons" ("The Family of William Claiborne Walton and Lucinda Muse," www.trakwest.com/zwal36.htm, retrieved Oct. 22, 2010).

4. S. H. Lewis to Lunsford Lewis, Jan. 22, 1868, Virginia Historical Society; Wayland, *History of Rockingham County*, 252. Wise was called as rector in 1866, as the parish began holding services in Port Republic and Harrisonburg on alternate Sundays. At first the parish's part-time rector had been, again, Samuel Hance Lewis's son-in-law, the Rev. James C. Wheat of Staunton. Along with their father, John F. Lewis and Samuel H. Lewis Jr. were on the new vestry, along with, among others, a cousin—Andrew Lewis of Harrisonburg—and two long-time family friends, Dr. George W. Kemper of Port Republic and Algernon S. Gray of Harrisonburg. John F. Lewis and Andrew Lewis were elected wardens. Samuel H. Lewis was named a delegate to one more diocesan convention, held in 1867 in Staunton (*Journal of the, Seventy-Fifth Annual Convention*, 111).

5. S. H. Lewis to Lunsford Lewis, Dec. 3, 1867, Virginia Historical Society; "Testimony of Charles H. Lewis," *Report of the Joint Committee*, 2:144; Lewis, *Second Biennial Report*, 187; State Government Records Collection, Secretary of the Commonwealth Records 1865–72, General Correspondence 1865, Appointment and Oath of the Secretary of the Commonwealth, Library of Virginia. In 1881, Pierpont changed the spelling of his last name from Pierpoint by dropping the second "i," which he no doubt never pronounced.

6. Bromberg, "Virginia Congressional Elections of 1865," *Virginia Magazine*, 80; "Charles H. Lewis to His Excellency And. Johnson" in Bergeron, *Papers of Andrew Johnson*, 340.

7. Testimony of Charles H. Lewis," *Report of the Joint Committee*, 2:144–45; Ambler, Francis H. Pierpont, 304; "Board of Visitors Minutes, July 5, 1865," University of Virginia Library, 176. The eight others named Visitor included noted Albemarle County Union Loyalist attorney and future judge Alexander Rives, whom the board elected its rector, or chief officer. Some appointments in Rockingham County were

suggested to Governor Pierpont in May 1865 by John F. Lewis, who was wasting no time in exercising his new influence as a steadfast Unionist. He urged the governor to appoint Dr. George K. Gilmer to the post of notary public. Dr. Gilmer at the time was, conveniently, in Alexandria—he had served in the Restored government—where he could be administered the oath. Upon his return to Rockingham, Dr. Gilmer could then, thought John F. Lewis, administer the required oaths to three other prospective notaries whose names Lewis was quick to suggest. One was his uncle Charles Lewis Jr., a schoolteacher for much of his life, who ultimately got the position (John F. Lewis to Gov. Pierpoint, May 4, 1865, Lunsford Lomax Lewis Papers, Huntington Library; Lowe, *Republicans and Reconstruction*, 80).

8. Confederate Papers, M346; Capron, "Virginia Iron Furnaces of the Confederacy," 16.

9. Capron, "Virginia Iron Furnaces of the Confederacy," 14; May, *My Augusta*, 413; "Testimony of Manasseh Blackburn," *Report of the Joint Committee*, 2:149. The furnace stack was rebuilt in 1874 and continued in blast for at least another four years, though ore continued to be mined and shipped elsewhere for smelting for much longer. The property was broken up and sold in 1905. The site of the stack is now within the boundaries of Shenandoah National Park. Archeological excavations have been conducted prior to planned restoration of remains of the furnace.

10. "John F. Lewis, Esq.," *RR*, Sept. 1, 1865, 2. Another declaration in his announcement was opposition to enforcement of the Monroe Doctrine. During the Civil War, the French government had installed Maximilian on the throne of Mexico, in defiance of the Monroe Doctrine's prohibition of European influence in the Western hemisphere. Having seen enough war, "I am emphatically for peace," stated Lewis.

11. John F. Lewis, Esq.," *RR*, Sept. 1, 1865, 2; Lewis, *Brief Narrative*, 63; Bromberg, "Virginia Congressional Elections of 1865," 81, 90; "Reply to Hon. A. H. H. Stuart's Card," *RR*, Oct. 6, 1865, 1.

12. Bromberg, "Virginia Congressional Elections of 1865," 90; Lowe, *Republicans and Reconstruction*, 44–45. Early on, John F. Lewis had gained a ringing endorsement from the *Richmond Whig*. He carried Page County by five votes, lost Albemarle by seven, took 45 percent of the Rockingham tally and close to that in Rockbridge, but lost by substantial margins in six other counties. In Rockingham County, he swept his home Port Republic precinct 71 to 28, a margin of 72 percent ("Rockingham Election," *RR*, Oct. 20 1865, 2; "For Congress–6th District," Nov. 3, 1865, 2).

13. "Testimony of Charles H. Lewis," *Report of the Joint Committee*, 2:145; Hildebrand, *Life and Times of John Brown Baldwin*, 192; Lowe, *Republicans and Reconstruction*, 46, 132. Underwood had not yet officially been seated in the Senate.

14. "Testimony of Charles H. Lewis," *Report of the Joint Committee*, 2:144–45; Lowe, "Testimony from the Old Dominion," 374, 380.

15. "Testimony of John F. Lewis," *Report of the Joint Committee*, 2:71.

16. "Testimony of Charles H. Lewis," *Report of the Joint Committee*, 2:147–48. Despite his disdain for the loyalty oath, Charles H. Lewis reported that Wise "declared his intention to comply strictly with the terms of his parole, and said that even now he loved the old Union better than most of those who made loud professions of devotion to it."

17. "Testimony of Charles H. Lewis," *Report of the Joint Committee*, 2:147.

18. "An Incendiary Scoundrel," *Valley Virginian*, Apr. 4, 1866, 2.

19. Lowe, *Republicans and Reconstruction*, 130–32. "I am very bitter in my feelings toward the secession party," John F. Lewis said early in 1866. "I have always been so. I always hated them as I hated the devil himself. But there is a class of persons that I hate more than the secessionists: that is the northern copperheads." He went on to criticize the copperhead *New York News*, a paper he called "one of our worst enemies. . . . I see a great many people in Staunton and the villages coming out of the post offices with the *News* in their hands. I think it has a very large circulation, and is doing

a great deal of mischief in our country." ("Testimony of John F. Lewis," *Report of the Joint Committee*, 2:73.)

20. John F. Lewis, "Carpet-Baggers and Permanent Settlers," *New York Times*, Jan. 4, 1873.

21. Baggett, *Scalawags*, 1–5.

22. Lowe, *Republicans and Reconstruction*, 59–60, 87.

23. "The Union State Convention," *Harrisonburg American Union*, May 26, 1866, 2. The term "delegate" was loosely applied. *American Union* editor George K. Gilmer wrote that the gathering was open to all those interested, and that he "went to the Alexandria convention simply as an individual, claiming to represent no one nor asking any favors of any one. We were admitted as a member of the convention as an act of courtesy, and so were our friends Lewis and Gray, who were with us on the occasion."

24. "The Union State Convention," *Harrisonburg American Union*, May 26, 1866, 2.

25. Lowe, *Republicans and Reconstruction*, 60. One issue was whether blacks should immediately be allowed to vote. John F. Lewis disagreed, but his qualifications on why they should be allowed to vote later were quickly misinterpreted. Rockingham delegate George K. Gilmer, who advocated Union Loyalist positions in his *Harrisonburg American Union*, took the *Staunton Spectator* to task for, "in its haste to make capital against Mr. Lewis," implying that on the issue of blacks voting John F. Lewis "had set his head against Negro suffrage through all time." Rather, wrote Gilmer, he "was opposed to it because he did not believe the Negro prepared for the proper use of the privilege of the elective franchise at present" ("The *Staunton Spectator* and John F. Lewis," *Harrisonburg American Union*, Jun. 9, 1866, 2).

26. Lowe, *Republicans and Reconstruction*, 74–75; Bromberg, "Virginia Congressional Elections," 80; "The *Alexandria Gazette* and the Late Union Convention," *Harrisonburg American Union*, May 26, 1866, 2; "The *Staunton Spectator* and John F. Lewis," *Harrisonburg American Union*, Jun. 9, 1866, 2. John F. Lewis's father, Samuel Hance Lewis, felt the same way: "He believed, to say the least, that in conferring universal Negro suffrage a great mistake was made; that the Negroes in their then condition were not qualified en masse to be voters, and that vastly more harm than good would result from their wholesale enfranchisement." (Lewis, *Brief Narrative*, 62.)

27. Lowe, *Republicans and Reconstruction*, 82, 84–86. Botts and other moderates thought a similar meeting held in Petersburg in April was too radical and limited in scope.

28. Lowe, *Republicans and Reconstruction*, 86; "To the Unconditional Union Men of Virginia," Lunsford Lomax Lewis Papers.

29. Frazier, *Family of John Lewis*, 88, 96. The second sons of Beverley and Charlotte Lewis Botts and Lunsford and Rosalie Botts Lewis were named for Samuel Hance Lewis. John Minor Botts's only other surviving child, Mary Minor Botts, married Walter Hoxsey, a Lewis in-law. The fourth Lewis married to a Republican in these years was John F. Lewis's oldest daughter, Nannie, who married John Ambler Smith of Richmond, a Republican state senator in 1869 who was soon elected to Congress.

30. Lowe, *Republicans and Reconstruction*, 72–73, 86, 88, 92–93.

31. Lowe, *Republicans and Reconstruction*, 126; "22 October 1867 Referendum," Rockingham County Ms. Election Records No. 427, Library of Virginia.

32. C. H. Lewis to Henry Wilson, Nov. 19, 1867, Henry Wilson Papers, Library of Congress. Lewis began in a roundabout way by referring to an earlier letter from Wilson and then outlined the situation: "I was gratified to be assured that you so fully appreciate the motives of the white loyal men of Virginia & understand so well the delicacy of our position, subjected, as we are, to the misconstruction of ignorant & rash men of our own party, & held responsible by the designing politicians of the rebel party—North [the copperheads] & South—for a condition of affairs here which, however exaggerated, is bad enough, and which we did all in our power to avert."

33. Lowe, *Republicans and Reconstruction*, 142–43, 144–45, 148.

34. Lowe, *Republicans and Reconstruction*, 158–59; Scott, *History of Orange County*, 162; "Lunsford Lomax Lewis," *Report of the Thirty-First Annual Meeting*, 98. Sheffey Lewis replaced a Conservative attorney who had held the job since 1831 and who in two years—after Reconstruction ended—was reinstated.

35. Lowe, *Republicans and Reconstruction*, 166–67.

36. Lowe, *Republicans and Reconstruction*, 167–68, 174–75. One important True Republican backer was William Mahone, a brigadier general under Robert E. Lee, who was seeking to consolidate Virginia's three railroads rather than have them fall under the control of the Baltimore & Ohio Railroad, such an important logistical element in the Union victory. From Lewiston, Charles H. Lewis continued working for the True Republican ticket (Charles H. Lewis to G. K. Gilmer, March 1869, Gilmer and Maguire Papers).

37. Lowe, *Republicans and Reconstruction*, 172; "To the Voters of the Sixth Congressional District of Virginia," Broadsides, Virginia Historical Society, Jun. 4, 1869.

38. Lowe, *Republicans and Reconstruction*, 177.

39. "To the Voters of the Sixth Congressional District of Virginia," Broadsides, Virginia Historical Society, Jun. 4, 1869.

40. Lewis, *Brief Narrative*, 65. Samuel Hance Lewis died of effects of a small cancerous growth on his cheek, which had bothered him for more than ten years and was surgically removed nearly two years before his death. One early treatment was applying a poultice of boiled clover blossoms (S. H. Lewis to Lunsford Lewis, Dec. 3, 1867, Lewis Family Papers, Virginia Historical Society; John Tayloe Lomax to S. H. Lewis, Nov. 15, 1859, Lewis Family Papers, Virginia Historical Society).

41. John F. Lewis was administrator for the Botts estate. (Feb. 23, 1869 receipt in Lunsford Lewis Papers.)

42. *New York World Almanac*, 78; J. C. Fletcher to Hamilton Fish, Secretary of State, Jun. 7, 1870, General Records of the Department of State 1790–1906, M-43 Roll 24.

43. Charles H. Lewis to the Hon. Hamilton Fish, Secretary of State, Jun. 16, 1870, General Records of the Department of State, Microcopy No. 43, Vol. 24, roll T-23.

Epilogue: To a New Century

1. Gallagher, ed., *Shenandoah Valley Campaign of 1864*, 241; Mills, *Southern Loyalists*, ix–x. Claims were usually allowed for items officially requested, though not for losses due to "military necessity." Outcomes were mixed on claims based on verbal agreements or general looting. Decisions were based on claimants' and witnesses' answers to 80 standing interrogatories, divided into subsections to be asked according to the category of person or claim being heard.

2. In 1871, Lunsford Lewis asked brother John F., then a U.S. senator, to check with claims commissioners in Washington to get the sense of the potential impact of testimony by Maj. Gen. W. S. Hancock, who could verify details of a client's claim. The claim, by Ella V. Gordon for $5,070, was ultimately disallowed (L. L. Lewis to John F. Lewis, Dec. 13, 1871 to John F. Lewis, *UCWE*, 5:1068–69; Mills, *Southern Loyalists*, 230).

3. "Gen. Samuel H. Lewis Estate Claim," *UCWE*, 5:313–35. Supporting payment material not published in *UCWE* is in the National Archives, Southern Claims Commission files, Claim 11227. Of his eleven surviving children, three were not yet adults by the end of the war, and were therefore not considered for claims purposes. Maj. Gen. Samuel Sprigg Carroll, who as a colonel the afternoon before the battle had sat on the portico of Lewiston and promised payment, is listed as a witness for the claim, though no testimony of his, if any, has been preserved.

4. "Samuel H. Lewis Jr. Claim," *UCWE*, 5:337–49; Mills, *Southern Loyalists*, 52; "Records of the Commissioners of Claims," National Archives Microfilm Publication

M87, Roll 13. Records of three receipts showing outright sale by Samuel H. Lewis Jr. of corn, straw, and flour to the Confederate Army were turned up after the claims decision, too late to have any effect on the outcome. The Mount Vernon Furnace claim file cannot be found in the National Archives.

5. Lowe, "John Francis Lewis," *American National Biography*, 13:585; Ramage, *Gray Ghost*, 272, 274–75, 277.

6. Smith, *Proceedings of the National Union Republican Convention*, 50, 54–55.

7. Charles H. Lewis to Hon. Hamilton Fish, Secretary of State, Oct. 24, 1872, General Records of the Department of State 1790–1906, M-43 Roll 24. On another occasion, a Naval officer who had met Sen. John F. Lewis told brother Charles that "he could have told by our faces that we were Union men if he had never heard of us before, there being an unmistakable expression of countenance that indicated that we could neither be 'hitched on' to what we did not approve or 'dragged out' of the course we choose to adopt" (Charles H. Lewis to Lou Dabney Lewis, Mar. 22, 1871, author's collection).

8. Charles H. Lewis to Lou Dabney Lewis, Mar. 22, 1871, author's collection. There is some indication that Charles H. Lewis spoke Portuguese.

9. Charles H. Lewis to Hon. Hamilton Fish, Secretary of State, Apr. 9, 1875, General Records of the Department of State, M-43 Roll 24; French, "Charles H. Lewis," S. Bassett French Collection. In reporting Charles H. Lewis's work on a history of Portugal, French puts the date of the loss at 1870. The 1870 flood, however, occurred in September, when Lewis was already in Lisbon and not living in his home on the Shenandoah's lower plain. Since it is more probable that he worked on the book after he had been in Portugal, the correct flood date is likely November 1877, when cattle, hogs, and sheep at low-lying Lynnwood were swept away and more than 100 barrels of flour were counted floating from the nearby mill ("Terrible Flood," *RR*, Nov. 29, 1877).

10. John F. Lewis to Williams C. Wickham, Jul. 26, 1873, author's collection; Lowe, "John Francis Lewis," American National Biography, 13:585.

11. Maddex, *Virginia Conservatives*, 95–96; Moore, "The Death of the Duel," 260–61. None of the improvements were made during the war, since the Fourteenth Amendment had required southern states to renounce their Confederate debts.

12. Moore, *Two Paths to the New South*, 70–73, 120–21; Maddex, *Virginia Conservatives*, 271–72.

13. Moore, *Two Paths to the New South*, 73, 120–21.

14. Moore, "The Death of the Duel," 259–60.

15. Moore, "The Death of the Duel," 266; "The Belligerant Virginians," New York Times, Sept. 20, 1881.

16. Moore, "The Belligerant Virginians," *New York Times*, Sept. 20, 1881; Moore, "Death of the Duel," 266–67.

17. Moore, "Death of the Duel," 266–67; Arritt, "Last Duel in Virginia." In 1882, John F. Lewis's son-in-law J. Ambler Smith, running as a Readjuster for the Richmond Congressional seat held by George D. Wise, publicly insulted the short-tempered Wise, and a challenge resulted. But for weapons Smith chose double-barreled shotguns at forty paces, and the duel never took place. Wise defeated Smith in the election (Moore, "Death of the Duel," 272–73).

18. Arritt, "Last Duel in Virginia"; "The Duel Fought at Last," *New York Times*, Jul. 1, 1883. Dr. Lewis Wheat was apparently forced from his post as anatomy instructor at the Virginia Medical College, run by a Funder-dominated board, for his Readjuster views. (Moore, "Battle for the Medical College," 160.)

19. "Lunsford Lomax Lewis," *Report of the Thirty-First Annual Meeting*, 98. Lunsford Lewis's first wife, Rosalie Botts, died in 1878. Five years later he married Janie Looney, daughter of Robert Looney of Memphis, Tennessee, a former Unionist who became a Confederate Army colonel and later developed mining interests in Mexico.

In the mid-1880s he was Tennessee's representative on the Democratic National Committee (Speer, *Sketches of Prominent Tennesseans*, 121–22).

20. Moore, "Death of the Duel," 274; John F. Lewis to G. K. Gilmer, Jun. 10, 1889, John F. Lewis to G. K. Gilmer, Apr. 3, 1890, John F. Lewis to G. K. Gilmer, Nov. 24, 1880, Gilmer and Maguire Papers. "Thomasite" was a Biblical reference to "Doubting Thomas."

21. John F. Lewis to G. K. Gilmer, Aug. 21, 1880, Gilmer and Maguire Papers; Wayland, *Virginia Valley Records*, 233; "Republican Mayor Elected," *New York Times*, Jul. 24, 1886; French, "Daniel Sheffey Lewis," "Beverly Botts Lewis," S. Bassett French Collection.

22. Moore, *Two Paths to the New South*, 82, 119–23.

23. *Report of the Thirty-First Annual Meeting*, 98–99; Theodore Roosevelt to Judge Lewis, Nov. 19, 1901, Lewis Family Papers, Virginia Historical Society.

24. "L. L. Lewis for Governor," *New York Times*, Aug. 10, 1905; Daryl Cumber Dance, *The Lineage of Abraham: The Biography of a Free Black Family in Charles City, Va.* (Richmond, D. C. Dance, 1998), excerpt cited Mar. 26, 2012 at www.africanaheritage.com/LineageofAbrahamexcerpt.asp.

25. Ferrell, *Claude A. Swanson*, 69; Larsen, *Montague of Virginia*, 111; Pulley, *Old Virginia Restored*, 131.

26. In the previous century, the Lewises were pleased that slavery had ended. When laws changed, they set aside their belief that blacks had been prematurely granted the right to vote, and worked with blacks in political harness. But John F. Lewis thought trying to integrate schools at that time would be going too far. In 1874 a black constituent wrote Senator Lewis on the subject, and was cautioned that his reach should not exceed his grasp. "It is known to every intelligent person that the white people have a large and increasing majority in Virginia, and in point of education and wealth are very far in advance of the colored population," Lewis responded. "It is also known that there is an inveterate prejudice entertained by a very large majority of its citizens against mixed schools." However, it was also common knowledge, he wrote, that the state's school fund was being "fairly and impartially disbursed, or, more correctly speaking, that the colored schools have been liberally cared for." Assuming that under the Republican administration of the early 1870s schools for blacks were indeed being equally funded, black children would thus have been benefitting as much as white children. But if laws were changed to require integrated schools, Lewis feared the Virginia legislature would simply refuse to appropriate money for any public schools, and black children would then be given no education at all. "Take care," John F. Lewis advised, "that in grasping at the shadow you do not lose the substance ("Senator Lewis on Civil Rights," *New York Times*, Jun. 18, 1874).

27. *Report of the Thirty-First Annual Meeting*, 99.

28. Frazier, *Family of John Lewis*, 320–25. Lewiston burned a second time, in 1925, and was replaced on a nearby site by a new and differently designed home—sold out of the family soon thereafter—oriented not toward the north but to the widened highway to the southeast. Although there are no known photographs of the original Lewiston, completed in 1827, those of the second home indicate its design corresponded with the original builder's plan, though the ell at the back was extended to the full width of the house. The portico seems of more recent design. Otherwise, thinks Shenandoah Valley architectural historian Ann E. McCleary, now at the University of West Georgia, most architectural details are more typical of homes built in 1827 than in 1875 ("Agreement between Samuel H. Lewis and Overton Gibson, Aug. 7, 1826," Lewis Family Papers, Virginia Historical Society; Ann E. McCleary to Lewis F. Fisher, Nov. 30, 2011).

29. Frazier, *Family of John Lewis*, 321, 324. The school operated from about 1890 to about 1912.

30. Lewis, "Drafters for Profit;" "John F. Lewis," *New York Times*, Sep. 3, 1895. Samuel H. Lewis Jr., 72 and said to have become hard of hearing, was carrying a jar of jelly to his ailing brother in February 1892 when he was struck by a fast freight train as he began to cross the tracks at the Lynnwood crossing. ("Samuel H. Lewis Sr. Instantly Killed," undated and unidentified Harrisonburg newspaper clipping, author's collection). Younger brother William M. Lewis, 43, also met a tragic end, in December 1878, when he was swept away and drowned while trying to cross the swollen river. John F. Lewis's financial affairs were in disarray at the time of his death. Lynnwood was sold a few years later—his family lived there until 1915—but in 1962 came back in the family for four decades and was restored by a great-grandson, Thomas B. Dilworth Jr. and his wife, Elizabeth Walker Dilworth (Frazier, *Family of John Lewis*, 310).

31. Maria H. Baldwin to Oliver P. Baldwin, Baldwin Family Papers. The undated letter's envelope bears a stamp issued in 1870, and the addressee died in 1878.

Bibliography

Ambler, Charles H. *Francis H. Pierpont, Union War Governor of Virginia and Father of West Virginia*. Chapel Hill: University of North Carolina Press, 1937.

_____. *Sectionalism in Virginia from 1776 to 1861*. Morgantown: West Virginia University Press, 2008.

The American Union. Harrisonburg, Va.: 1866–67.

Arritt, Gay. "Last Duel in Virginia 75 Years Ago Today." *Covington Virginian*, Jun. 30, 1958, 6.

Ayers, Edward L., and Gary W. Gallagher and Andrew J. Torget, eds. *Crucible of the Civil War: Virginia from Secession to Commemoration*. Charlottesville: University of Virginia Press, 2006.

Baggett, James Alex. *The Scalawags: Southern Dissenters in the Civil War*. Baton Rouge: Louisiana State University Press, 2002.

Baldwin Family Papers, 1836–1970, Virginia Historical Society, Richmond, Va.

Beale, Howard K. *The Diary of Edward Bates, 1859–1866*. rep. New York: Da Capo Press, 1971.

Bergeron, Paul H. T*he Papers of Andrew Johnson*. Knoxville: University of Tennessee Press, 1989.

Berkey, Jonathan M. "Rockingham Rebellion." *Encyclopedia Virginia*. Library of Virginia, ed. Brendan Wolfe. 8 Dec. 2010. Virginia Foundation for the Humanities. 15 Mar. 2010 www.EncyclopediaVirginia.org/Rockingham_Rebellion.

Blair, William. *Virginia's Private War: Feeding Body and Soul in the Confederacy, 1861–1865*. New York: Oxford University Press, 1998.

Blake, Nelson Morehouse. *William Mahone of Virginia: Soldier and Political Insurgent*. Richmond: Garrett & Massie, 1935.

Brady, Tate Thompson, Papers, 1971–1992. Virginia Historical Society, Richmond, Va.

Bromberg, Alan B. "The Virginia Congressional Elections of 1865: A Test of Southern Loyalty." *Virginia Magazine of History and Biography*, 84 (1976), 75–98.

Bruggeman, Seth C. "The Shenandoah River Gundalow: Reusable Boats in Virginia's Nineteenth-Century River Trade." *Virginia Magazine of History and Biography*, 118:4 (December 2010), 315–49.

Bynum, Victoria E. *The Long Shadow of the Civil War: Southern Dissent and Its Legacies*. Chapel Hill: University of North Carolina Press, 2010.

Cappon, Lester J. *Virginia Newspapers 1821–1935, A Bibliography with Historical Introduction and Notes*. New York: D. Appleton–Century Co., 1936.

Capron, John D., Collection. Knight-Capron Library, Lynchburg College, Lynchburg, Va.

_____. "Virginia Iron Furnaces of the Confederacy." *Virginia Cavalcade*, 17:2 (Autumn 1967), 10–18.

Catalog of the Officers and Alumni of Washington and Lee University, Lexington, Virginia, 1749–1888. Baltimore: John Murphy & Co., 1888.

Cheney, Newel. *History of the Ninth Regiment, New York Volunteer Cavalry. War of 1861 to 1865*. Poland Center, N.Y.: n.p., 1901.

Colt, Margaretta Barton. *Defend the Valley: A Shenandoah Valley Family in the Civil War.* New York: Onion Books, 1994.

Confederate Papers Relating to Citizens or Business Firms. M346, National Archives, Washington, D.C.

Cowell, M[ark] W. [Jr.]. "Some Notes on Thomas Lewis's Will." *Rockingham Recorder,* 3:3 (April 1985), 15–30.

Crofts, Daniel W. *Reluctant Confederates: Upper South Unionists in the Secession Crisis.* Chapel Hill: University of North Carolina Press, 1989.

Current, Richard Nelson. *Lincoln's Loyalists: Union Soldiers from the Confederacy.* Boston: Northeastern University Press, 1992.

Dabney, Virginius. *Virginia: The New Dominion.* New York: Doubleday & Company, 1971.

Downs, Janet Baugher, and Earl J. Downs with Pat Turner Ritchie, comps. *Mills of Rockingham County.* 3 vols. Dayton, Va.: Harrisonburg–Rockingham Historical Society, 1997–2000.

du Bellet, Louise Pecquet. *Some Prominent Virginia Families.* Lynchburg: J. P. Bell Company, 1907.

Dyer, Thomas G. *Secret Yankees: The Union Circle in Confederate Atlanta.* Baltimore: Johns Hopkins University Press, 1999.

Eckenrode, H. J. *The Political History of Virginia During the Reconstruction.* Baltimore: The Johns Hopkins Press, 1904.

Ellis, Sarah E. "Mount Vernon Furnace." *Quarterly Bulletin of the Archeological Society of Virginia,* 66:1 (March 2011), 1–10.

Faulkner, Charles James, Papers. Virginia Historical Society, Richmond, Va.

Ferrell, Henry C. Jr. *Claude A. Swanson of Virginia: A Political Biography.* Kentucky: University of Kentucky Press, 1985.

Fischer, David Hackett, and James C. Kelly. *Bound Away: Virginia and the Westward Movement.* Charlottesville: University of Virginia Press, 2000.

Frazier, Irvin, comp., text by Mark W. Cowell Jr., edited by Lewis F. Fisher. *The Family of John Lewis, Pioneer.* San Antonio: Fisher Publications Inc., 1985.

French, S. Bassett. S. Bassett French Biographical Sketches Collection, Library of Virginia Digital Collection. lvaimage.lib.va.us/collections/BF.html.

Freehling, William W., and Craig M. Simpson, eds. *Showdown in Virginia: The 1861 Convention and the Fate of the Union.* Charlottesville: University of Virginia Press, 2010.

Gallagher, Gary W., ed. *The Shenandoah Valley Campaign of 1862.* Chapel Hill: University of North Carolina Press, 2003.

_____. *The Shenandoah Valley Campaign of 1864.* Chapel Hill: The University of North Carolina Press, 2006.

General Records of the Department of State, Despatches from United States Ministers to Portugal, 1790–1906, Microcopy No. 43. Vol. 24, roll T-23, Jul. 16, 1869–Jun. 16, 1874; vol. 25, roll T-24, Jul. 6, 1874–Feb. 5, 1876. Washington: National Archives, National Archives and Records Service, General Services Administration, 1962.

Gilmer, George Rockingham. *Sketches of Some of the First Settlers of Upper Georgia, of the Cherokees and the Author.* New York, 1855. rep. Baltimore, Genealogical Publishing Company, 1999.

Gilmer and Maguire Papers. Virginia Historical Society, Richmond, Va.

Goode, G. Browne. *Virginia Cousins.* Richmond: J. W. Randolph & English, 1887.

Grattan, Peachy R. *Reports of Cases Decided in the Supreme Court of Appeals of Virginia,* 32. Charlottesville: Michie Company, 1900.

Greiner, Anthony. "Navigation and Commerce on the Shenandoah River of Virginia." *The Log of Mystic Seaport*, 42:2 (Summer 1990), 42–45.

Harris, John T., Papers 1771–1937, James Madison University Carrier Library Special Collections, Harrisonburg, Va..

Harrisonburg American Union. Harrisonburg, Va. 1866–67.

Heatwole, John L. *The Burning: Sheridan in the Shenandoah Valley*. Charlottesville: Rockbridge Publishing, 1998.

Hildebrand, John R. *The Life and Times of John Brown Baldwin, 1820–1873*. Staunton: Lot's Wife Publishing for the Augusta County Historical Society, 2008.

Hotchkiss, Jedediah. *Make Me a Map of the Valley: The Civil War Journals of Stonewall Jackson's Topographer*. Dallas: Southern Methodist University Press, 1973.

_____. "The Shenandoah Valley Railroad and the Mineral and Other Resources of the Country Tributary to It." *The Virginias, A Mining, Industrial, and Scientific Journal*, 1:3 (March 1880), 36–37.

Isaac, Rhys. *The Transformation of Virginia, 1749–1790*. Chapel Hill: University of North Carolina Press, 1982.

Jackson, Donald, and Dorothy Twohig, eds. *The Diaries of George Washington: 4, 1784–June 1786*. Charlottesville: University Press of Virginia, 1978.

Journal of the Convention of the Protestant Episcopal Church in the Diocese of Virginia. Richmond: B. R. Wren, 1837 1843–51, 1856, 1867.

Journal of the House of Delegates of the Commonwealth of Virginia, 1841. Richmond: Commonwealth of Virginia, 1842.

Julienne, Marianne E. and Brent Tarter. "The Virginia Ordinance of Secession." *Virginia Magazine of History and Biography*, 119:2 (2011), 154–81.

Kimball, Gregg D. "Militias, Politics and Patriotism: Virginia and Union in Antebellum Richmond." *Virginia Cavalcade*, 46:4 (Autumn 2000), 158–177.

Koons, Kenneth E., and Warren R. Hofstra, eds. *After the Backcountry: Rural Life in the Great Valley of Virginia 1800–1900*. Knoxville: University of Tennessee Press, 2000.

Krick, Robert K. *Conquering the Valley: Stonewall Jackson at Port Republic*. New York: William Morrow and Company, 1996.

Lambert, Darwin. *The Undying Past of Shenandoah National Park*. Luray, Va.: Shenandoah Natural History Association, 1989.

Larsen, William. *Montague of Virginia*. Baton Rouge: Louisiana State University Press, 1965.

Lesley, J. P. *The Iron Manufacturer's Guide to the Furnaces, Forges and Rolling Mills of the United States*. New York: John Wiley, 1859.

"Lewis, Charles Hance." *National Cyclopaedia of American Biography* 12:121. George Derby and James Terry White eds. New York: J. T. White, 1892.

Lewis, John F. [Jr.] "Drafters for Profit," *The National Stockman and Farmer*. Pittsburgh: Stockman–Farmer Publishing Co., Jan. 9, 1913.

Lewis, Lunsford Lomax. *A Brief Narrative, Written for His Grandchildren*. Richmond: Richmond Press Inc., 1915.

_____. Papers, 1865–1881. Robert Alonzo Brock Collection, Huntington Library, San Marino, Calif.

Lewis, S. H. "Speech Delivered Before a Convention of the Temperance Societies of Rockingham County at Harrisonburg on the 26 of September 1835." Lewis Family Papers, 1749–1920, Virginia Historical Society, Richmond, Va.

Lewis, Gen. Samuel H., and Samuel Lewis Jr. War Claims, 1872–1878. National Archives, Military Reference Branch, Washington, D.C.

Lewis, Virgil A. *Second Biennial Report of the Department of Archives and History of the State of West Virginia*, 2. Charleston: West Virginia Dept. of Archives and History, 1913.

Lewis Family File. Harrisonburg-Rockingham Historical Society, Harrisonburg, Va.

Lewis Family File. Society of Port Republic Preservationists, Port Republic, Va.

Lewis Family Papers. Author's collection.

Lewis Family Papers, 1749–1920, Augusta and Rockingham Counties, Virginia. Virginia Historical Society, Richmond, Va.

Lomax, Edward Lloyd. *Genealogy of the Virginia Family of Lomax*. Chicago: Rand McNally Co., 1913.

Lowe, Richard. "John Francis Lewis." *American National Biography*, ed. John A. Garraty and Mark C. Carnes. New York: Oxford University Press, 1999, 13:584–85.

_____. *Republicans and Reconstruction in Virginia, 1856–70*. Charlottesville: University Press of Virginia, 1991.

_____. "Testimony from the Old Dominion Before the Joint Committee on Reconstruction." *Virginia Magazine of History and Biography*, 104:3 (Summer 1996), 373–98.

Maddex, Jack. *Virginia Conservatives, 1867–1879: A Study in Reconstruction Politics*. Chapel Hill: University of North Carolina Press, 1970.

Mahon, Michael G. *The Shenandoah Valley, 1861–1865: The Destruction of the Granary of the Confederacy*. Mechanicsburg, Pa.: Stackpole Books, 1999.

Malone, Dumas. *Jefferson and his Time*. Boston: Little, Brown, 1948.

Martinsburg Gazette. Martinsburg, Va. 1847–48.

May, Clarence Edward. *Life Under Four Flags in North River Basin of Virginia*. Verona, Va.: McClure Printing Co., 2nd ed., 1982.

_____. *My Augusta*. Virginia Beach: Good Printers, 1987.

May, George Elliott. *Port Republic: The History of a Shenandoah Valley Town*. Staunton: Lot's Wife Publishing, 2002.

McCluskey, Turk. "Rich Land, Poor Prospects: Real Estate and the Formation of a Social Elite in Augusta County, Virginia, 1738–1770." *Virginia Magazine of History and Biography*, 97 (July 1990, 449–86.

Meade, Bishop [William]. *Old Churches, Ministers and Families of Virginia*. Philadelphia: J. B. Lippincott Company, 1906.

Mills, Gary B. *Southern Loyalists in the Civil War: The Southern Claims Commission*. Baltimore: Genealogical Publishing Co., 1994.

Moore, James T. "Battle for the Medical College: Physicians, Politicians and the Courts, 1882–1883." *Virginia Cavalcade*, 31:3 (Winter 1982), 158–67.

_____. "The Death of the Duel: The Code Duello in Readjuster Virginia 1879–1883." *Virginia Magazine of History and Biography*, 83:3 (July 1975), 259–76.

_____. *Two Paths to the New South: The Virginia Debt Controversy, 1870–1883*. Lexington: University of Kentucky Press, 1974.

Murphy, Terrence V. *10th Virginia Infantry*. Lynchburg: H.E. Howard, 1989.

New York Times. New York 1851–95.

New York World Almanac. New York: New York World, 1871.

Permanent Temperance Documents of the American Temperance Society. Boston: Seth Bliss and Perkins, Marvin and Co., 1835.

Peyton, J. Lewis. *History of Augusta County, Virginia*. Staunton: Samuel M. Yost & Son, 1882.

_____, comp. *Memoir of John Howe Peyton in Sketches by His Contemporaries, Together with Some of his Public and Private Letters, etc., Also a Sketch of Ann M. Peyton*. Staunton: A. B. Blackburn & Co., 1894.

The Preston and Virginia Papers of the Draper Collection of Manuscripts. State Historical Society of Wisconsin, Madison, Wis.

Pulley, Raymond. *Old Virginia Restored*. Charlottesville: University Press of Virginia, 1968.

Ramage, James A. *Gray Ghost: The Life of John Singleton Mosby*. Lexington: University of Kentucky Press, 1999.

Report of the Joint Committee on Reconstruction at the First Session Thirty-Ninth Congress, 2: Virginia, North Carolina, South Carolina. Washington: Government Printing Office, 1866.

Report of the Thirty-First Annual Meeting of the Virginia State Bar Association. Richmond: Richmond Press, 1920.

Reese, George H., ed. *Proceedings of the Virginia State Convention of 1861, February 13–May 1*. Richmond: Virginia State Library, 1965.

Rockingham Recorder. Rockingham County Historical Society/Harrisonburg-Rockingham Historical Society. Harrisonburg, Va. 1945–85.

Rockingham Register. Harrisonburg, Va. 1859–65.

Rodes, David S., and Norman R. Wenger, comps., Emmert F. Bittinger, ed. *Unionists and the Civil War Experience in the Shenandoah Valley, 5*. Rockport, ME: Penobscot Press, 2003–09.

Scott, W. W. *A History of Orange County Virginia*. Richmond: Everett Waddey & Co., 1907.

Secretary of the Commonwealth Records, 1865–1872, Accession 38130, State Government Records Collection, The Library of Virginia, Richmond, Va.

Shade, William G. *Democratizing the Old Dominion: Virginia and the Second Party System, 1824–1861*. Charlottesville: University of Virginia Press, 1997.

Shanks, Henry T. *The Secession Movement in Virginia, 1847–1861*. Richmond: Garrett & Massie, 1934.

The Shenandoah River Atlas. Front Royal, Va.: Friends of the Shenandoah River, 1997.

Smith, Francis H., reporter. *Proceedings of the National Union Republican Convention Held at Philadelphia, June 5 and 6, 1872*. Washington: Gibson Brothers, 1872.

Southern Literary Messenger. Richmond, Va., Sept. 1842, Jan. 1844.

Speer, William S. *Sketches of Prominent Tennesseans*. 1888, rep. Baltimore: Genealogical Publishing Co., 2003.

Staunton Spectator and Advertiser. Staunton, Va. 1843–49.

Swank, James M. *History of the Manufacture of Iron in all Ages, and Particularly in the United States from Colonial Times to 1891*. Philadelphia: American Iron and Steel Association, 1892.

Storey, Margaret. *Loyalty and Loss: Alabama's Unionists in the Civil War and Reconstruction*. Baton Rouge: Louisiana State University Press, 2004.

Strayer, Clara. Diary Transcript. National Register file—Bogota. Virginia Department of Historic Resources, Richmond, Va.

Strother, David Hunter. *A Virginia Yankee in the Civil War: The Diaries of David Hunter Strother*. Chapel Hill: University of North Carolina Press, 1961.

Tyler, Lyon G., ed. *Encyclopedia of Virginia Biography*. New York: Lewis Historical Publishing Co., 1915.

_____. *Men of Mark in Virginia: Ideals of American Life*. Washington: Men of Mark Publishing Company, 1907.

USDA Forest Service. "The Historic Iron and Charcoaling Industries in Virginia's Shenandoah Valley," Roanoke: George Washington & Jefferson National Forests, 2012.

Waddell, Joseph A. *Annals of Augusta County Virginia, from 1726 to 1971*. Staunton: C. Russell Caldwell, 1902.

The War of the Rebellion: A Compilation of the Official Records of the Union and Confederate Armies. Washington: Government Printing Office, 1880–1901.

Wayland, John Walter. *A History of Rockingham County, Virginia*. Harrisonburg, Va.: Ruebush-Elkins Co., 1912.

_____. *Men of Mark and Representative Citizens of Harrisonburg and Rockingham County, Virginia*. rep. Baltimore: Clearfield Publishing Company, 2009.

_____. *Virginia Valley Records: Genealogical and Historical Materials of Rockingham County*. Strasburg: Shenandoah Publishing House Inc., 1930.

Wheat, Ella Wood Rutherfoord 1852–1927, Papers. Virginia Historical Society, Richmond, Va.

Whisonant, Robert C. "Geology and History of the Civil War Iron Industry in the New River–Cripple Creek District of Southwestern Virginia." *Virginia Minerals* 44:4 (November 1998), 25–33.

Wilson, Henry, Papers, 1812–75. Manuscript Division, Library of Congress, Washington, D.C.

Wineman, Bradford A. "Whig Party in Virginia." *Encyclopedia Virginia*, ed. Brendan Wolfe. Nov. 9, 2010. (Virginia Foundation for the Humanities, May 28, 2010) www.EncyclopediaVirginia.org/Whig_Party_in_Virginia.

Wyatt-Brown, Bertram. *Southern Honor: Ethics and Behavior in the Old South*. Oxford University Press, 1982.

Photo Credits

Battles and Leaders of the Civil War (New York: Century Co., 1884), 31

Richard H. Dilworth, 18, 79

Huntington Library, San Marino, Cal., BR Box 143(1) fld. 6, 68

Library of Congress, Geography and Map Division, ii; Civil War Photographs Collection, 21, 29, 32, 65; Jedediah Hotchkiss Papers, 46; Morgan Collection, 50, 55; Brady-Handy Collection, 62

Library of Virginia, Secretary of the Commonwealth Records, 57 (above left and below)

Lynchburg College Library, Capron Collection, 44

Langhorne Lewis McCarthy, 54

Society of Port Republic Preservationists, 34

Virginia Historical Society, 2 (above), 71 (left)

Index

86, 108n25, 111n26; hosts Stonewall Jackson, 28–29, 36; threatened, 23, 26, 40; operates iron furnace, 40–48, 60, 103n21, 103n27, 104n30; immediate postwar, 67, 107n7, 107n19, 108n23; congressional candidate, 61–62, 71, 72, 107n10, 107n12; aids former Confederates, 63; attitude on carpetbaggers, 64; John M. Botts ally, 67, 69, 109n41; lieutenant governor, 71–72, 79 80, 81; U. S. senator, 72, 77, 78, 109n2; vice presidential nominee, 77; U.S. marshal, 78, 81; death, 84–85, 112n30

Lewis, John F., Jr., 80, 84

Lewis, Lunsford L., viii, 10, 65, 69, 110n19; education, 1, 55, 60, 96n5; Union Loyalist, 1, 40; in wartime, 27, 37, 50, 53–55, 103n21; John M. Botts aide, 69, 73; in Culpeper, 69, 70, 73, 75–76, 82, 109n2; duel with Peyton Wise, 80; Supreme Court, 81; U. S. attorney, 82–83, 84; congressional candidate, 82; gubernatorial candidate, 83; death, 84

Lewis, M. Botts, 81, 105n8

Lewis, Margaret Lynn, 2, 5

Lewis, Martha Fry, 10

Lewis, Nancy C., 9, 94n18

Lewis, Rachel Miller, 94n18

Lewis, Rosalie Botts, 65, 69, 73

Lewis, Samuel H., 9–10, 43, 67–69, 84, 94n24, 96n7, 97n4; early life and character, 1–2, 5; education, 7, 92n12; Episcopal Church, 2, 10–11, 94n23, 106n4; slavery and blacks, 10, 13, 38, 59, 94n21, 108n26, 111n26; militia, 11, 14, 97n22, 103n22; state legislator, 11–12; county judge and sheriff, 12; temperance, 12, 95n28; Union Loyalist, vii–viii, 1, 12, 13, 28, 95n1; in wartime, 37–38, 52, 99n11; hosts Stonewall Jackson, 28; postwar, 60, 67; death, 73, 109n40; estate war claim, 75–76, 109n3–4

Lewis, Samuel H., Jr., 67, 69, 76–77, 84, 106n4, 109n4, 112n30; slavery, 13; militia, 26–27, 98n1; Union Loyalist, 26, 40; in wartime, 25–27, 31, 32, 33,

50; war claim, 76–77, 99n11

Lewis, Serena Sheffey, 17, 36

Lewis, Thomas, 2–4, 5, 6–7, 92n6, 93n14

Lewis, Thomas (brother of Samuel H.), 2, 5, 7, 92n12, 100n17

Lewis, William, 92n5

Lewis, William M., 27, 35, 54, 60, 76 112n30; Confederate service, 27, 53, 105n15

Lewis mill, 3, 7, 17, 84, 101n8; 110n9; in wartime, 28, 51, 105n8

Lewiston, 11, 67, 94n20; construction and reconstruction, 9, 84–85, 93n17, 111n28; operations, 10, 17, 53, 59; in wartime, 25, 28, 30–31, 32, 33–35, 37, 38, 50, 52; Jackson's headquarters, 27

Lewiston Home School, 84, 111n29

Liberty Furnace, 44

Liggett, Jacob N., 19, 69

Lincoln, Abraham, 13, 16–17, 20, 22, 56, 96n12; relatives in Rockingham County, 97n22

Lomax, John T., 10, 14, 94n21, 96n5

Lomax, Lunsford L., 53, 105n14

Lynnwood, 3, 4, 59, 110n9, 112n30; construction, 5; in wartime, 32–33, 35, 36–37, 106n3; community, 84

Madison, Agatha Strother, 3, 5

Madison, James, 4, 5

Madison, John, 3, 5, 30

Mahone, William, 79, 81, 109n36

Maiden, William D., 39, 40–41, 52, 101n6

Margaret Jane Furnace. *See* Mount Vernon Furnace

Marshall, John, 12

Martinsburg, 14–15

Martinsburg Gazette, 15

Maupin, Tyre, 15–16

Maupin, William A., 25, 26

McKenzie, Lewis, 57

Meade, William, 2, 5, 10–11

Meason, Horatio B., 103n22

Mennonites and Brethren, 28, 39–40

Merritt, Wesley, 51–52

Miller, George, 47, 52

Miller, Henry, 41, 102n11

Miller, John, 42–43, 102n11, 102n18–19